# GROWING UP IN WILLIAMSBURG

## FROM THE DEPRESSION
## TO PEARL HARBOR

# GROWING UP IN WILLIAMSBURG

## FROM THE DEPRESSION TO PEARL HARBOR

by

## ED BELVIN

Illustrated by the author

Belvin

Printed by THE VIRGINIA GAZETTE INC.
Williamsburg

DEDICATION

To the long-time residents
of Williamsburg

# ACKNOWLEDGMENTS

I am grateful for the assistance of many people who furnished material for this volume. Special thanks must go to those who provided photographs, documents, information and advice. These include Mr. James Bowery, Mr. Lawrence Caldwell, Mr. Angelo Costas, Mr. Robert Gilley, Mr. Jack Goodwin, Mr. and Mrs. Charles Hunter, Mr. Martin Kline, Mr. William Molineux, Mr. Thomas Moyles, Mr. and Mrs. Lort Nightengale, Mrs Julia Oxrieder, Mr. Clarence Page, Rev. Thomas Pugh, Deacon M. O. Smith, Rev. J. B. Tabb, and Mr. George Wright, all of Williamsburg, and Mrs. Kitty Underwood of Yorktown.

I am especially indebted to Mrs. Julia Oxrieder and Dr. Carlton Casey for reading the manuscript and offering helpful suggestions. Also of great value was the majority of photographs used which were provided by Mr. Everett Johnston, nephew of the photographer Clyde Holmes. Credit is given under each of the other photographs. Some of the photographs are through the courtesy of the Daily Press and the kind interest of Mr. Will Molineux. Some of the research was done from filmed issues of the Virginia Gazette.

Cows on the Campus by Parke Rouse, Jr. was a great help as a reference for basic information and helped inspire me to write about Williamsburg.

Mrs. Barbara Dike of the Eastern State Medical Library and Miss Margaret Cooke of the William and Mary Library were also very helpful with my research as was Mr. Gordon Vliet and his staff of the College Alumni Society.

Mr. Warren Funke, Jr. provided the Peachy coat-of-arms and Mr. Jack Webb helped with the typing. Both are from Williamsburg.

Two of my informants have passed away since my interview with them. They are Miss Mary Wall Christian and Mr. William Person, Sr.

Others who searched their memories and provided information were Mr. W. V. Atkinson, Mrs. Baxter Bell, Sr., Mr. E. S. Bingley, Sr., Mrs. Gerald Bracey, Mr. Jeff Carter, Mr. Clarence Douglas, Mrs. Virginia Downey, Mr. Frank Dunn, Miss Jeanne Etheridge, Mr. George Farthing, Mr. Willard S. Gilley, Mr. Leonard Graves, Mr. Forrest Griffin, Mr. and Mrs. Albert Hunt, Sr., Mr. Jess Jackson, Mrs. Virginia Jones, Dr. Janet Kimbrough, Dean J. Wilfred Lambert, Dr. and Mrs. Charles Marsh, Mrs. Emma Mae Newcombe, Mrs. Elva Orr, Mr. Walter Owens, Mr. J. C. Palmer, Mrs. Thelma Pedersen, Miss Alice Person, Mr. George Pitts, Mr. and Mrs. Steve Sacalis, Miss Betsy Sacalis, Mr. Aubrey Skillman, Mrs. Margaret McSweeny, and Mrs. A. T. Vaughn, all of Williamsburg, and Mr. Joseph Carlton and Mrs. Mabel Sawyer of Toano.

Ed. Belvin

# CONTENTS

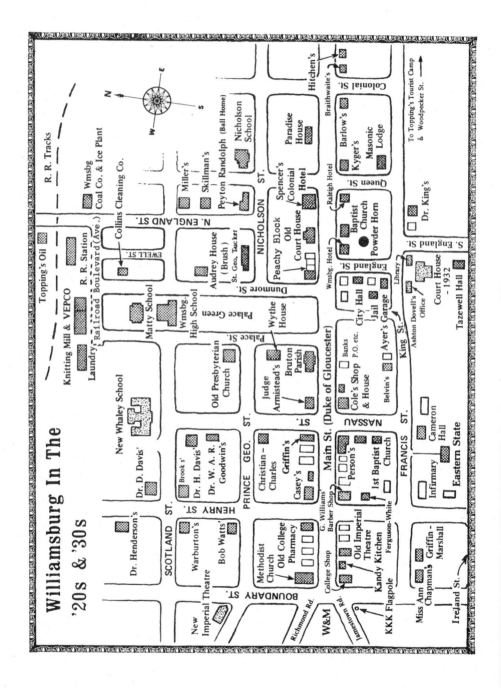

# Williamsburg In The
## '20s & '30s

PREFACE

This book has been written hopefully to fill a gap
in the information available about Williamsburg. A great
deal has been printed about the little city, from its
colonial history, through its restoration and finally about
its place as a unique small college town in today's
Virginia. There didn't seem to be anything available about
what it was like to grow up in this unusual place, at
least not during the Depression or the Restoration. Thus,
I decided to tackle the task.

Only a few experiences came to mind at first, but
as I searched the recesses of my memory and talked to
relatives and friends, more and more events and people came
rushing forth out of the past.

Most of my growing up in Williamsburg took place
in the 1930's. As in other small towns the times were more
gentle than today. The pace of life was slower. Everyone
knew everyone else. Crime was never much of a problem. My
family never locked our doors at night in spite of our
proximity to Eastern State Hospital. The Great Depression
was upon the land but Williamsburg was not as badly affected
as other areas. There were, since colonial days, the
College of William and Mary and Eastern State Hospital to
provide a source of employment for a few hundred people.
The Williamsburg Restoration, conceived in 1926, began to be
felt as an economic force by the '30s. It thereby became
the third institution tied to the colonial past of the
little city.

The story presented here covers the school years
of this writer from 1929 to 1941. It begins with the year
of the Great Depression and goes through the year of the
attack on Pearl Harbor. Many changes took place during

this thirteen-year period. The greatest change was the appearance of Williamsburg from a typical, somewhat shabby small town to a reborn colonial city (Williamsburg became a city in 1722). With this change in appearance came world renown, as the story of its glorious past was told to the world.

Part of the publicity necessary to let the world know what was happening in Williamsburg came from the aura of the Rockefeller wealth. However, from whatever the source, its fame has brought people from around the world to see the restored city. Williamsburg has become a convention center, attracting groups from all over our country. Many foreign leaders coming to Washington, D.C. on government business stop in Williamsburg.

I have tried to present a glimpse of the way things were in the little city while I was growing up during The Depression and The Restoration. It is probable that not everyone will agree with every-thing stated herein. I intended to mention the location of Lawson's Shoe Shop on Main Street near the Cole Shop but I found that other people remem-bered it in two other locations. Again, on the map is shown Railroad Boulevard as remembered by one person while others remembered it as Railroad Street and Railroad Avenue. Existing maps don't name it.

Since I wanted to view the past only with fondness, I have made an effort to avoid contro-versial subjects. However, I felt it necessary to describe the KKK flagpole presentation to William and Mary and to mention sterilization at Eastern State Hospital. As regards racial terms, "Negros" was used but "colored" seemed to be the term with which both Black and White were more comfortable. "Black" was not used until recent years.

Chapter 1

## IN THE BEGINNING

My earliest memories are of the preschool years living in what we called "The Peachy House." This is the present James Geddy House and Shop located on the eastern corner of Palace Green and Duke of Gloucester Street in Williamsburg. We called it "The Peachy House" because it was owned by the Peachy family. Duke of Gloucester Street was called by most people "Main Street." It was in this house that my family lived when I became old enough to attend school. A short walk from home led me to the Williamsburg High School, where most of the grades were taught. The remainder of the grades were taught in the Matty School (also spelled Mattey). On the area covered by these two schools now stands the Governor's Palace. The year was 1929. It was a memorable year for me in more ways than one. Most of the usual childhood diseases descended upon me in the first year of school causing me to miss so much time that I was to repeat the first grade, but in a brand new Matthew Whaley School. The old schools were demolished to build the Governor's Palace on its original site.

"The Restoration" as Colonial Williamsburg was first called was just getting started and I well remember watching the two narrow strips of Main Street being torn up to form the single street of today. The telephone poles and lines were removed and the lines were put underground. This was in 1932.

In my second year of school, my family moved to a house on Francis Street, not far from where we lived on Main Street. I was still close enough to walk to school which I did for all of the eleven years that I attended until graduation.

The new location on Francis Street was on the
edge of what we called "The Bottom," a ravine which
begins just south of Main Street.  It crosses Francis
Street and continues south along the present Parkway
toward the James River.  Many enjoyable days were spent
in this bottom by me, my brothers and my sister.
It was a haven for birds and other small wildlife.  I
believe it was this environment which caused me to
become a life-long nature lover.

There were two unusual specimens living in the
bottom.  They certainly were unusual to find in the
middle of town.  First, there were crayfish or crawfish as we called them which we dug out of the soft
ground and displayed to our friends.  Years later we
learned that some people ate crawfish but we never even
considered this.  Then there were stinging weeds or net-
tles which I have seldom seen elsewhere.  We learned of
their sting the hard way.  The sting was not quite as
severe as the more well-known jelly fish.

Beside our yard was a small walled graveyard.
In it were several headstones, most bearing the name
Cole.  On the far side of the bottom was another grave-
yard of equal size with headstones bearing the name
Maupin.  The dates were all in the nineteenth century.

Across the street from our house was the exercise yard for the women of Eastern State Hospital.  We
were told to stay away from "the crazy people," but as
we got to know some of the patients we lost all fear of
them.  The wild ones were not allowed out unattended
then as now, but we saw some strange sights as you can
well imagine.  The women were allowed out of the buildings into the yard several hours each day and I can

still seem to hear the nurses and attendants calling,
"Come on ladies, let's go in!" When we had relatives
or friends visiting, some of them would ask to "go see
the crazy people." We could see the women from our
front porch but a high board fence eliminated contact
with them and made conversation difficult.  So we would
walk or ride around the corner to South Henry Street
where the men's quarters were close to the street.  We
talked to some of the men through the windows since
there were always some who were anxious to talk.  Many
would say, "I'm not crazy, my wife put me in here."  Or
some would say, "Those doctors ganged up on me."  Many
had interesting things to say.

As I watched the buildings being reconstructed
or restored as the restoration of the city proceeded, I
began to be somewhat aware of how important our little
town was becoming.  History was not one of my favorite
subjects in school but much of the history of the
Williamsburg area was instilled in me.  I was more
impressed, however, by the people I met at school and
in town than by any of the leaders of colonial society.

The most memorable character I recall was an
aging man who was different from any one I had ever met.
We disrespectfully called him "Old Man Nelson," but not
to his face.  In later years I learned that his name was
Peyton Randolph Nelson, a descendant of the Yorktown
Nelsons and other prominent citizens of colonial Virginia.

His appearance was striking to say the least.
He had a full white beard, like Santa Claus, we thought.
We never saw him dressed in anything but work clothes,
consisting of plain blue or gray shirts and pants.  In
summer, he shed the shirt, revealing the upper part of
his long johns.  He always wore gloves, but never a
coat or hat, not even in the coldest weather.  He kept
a few cows and would drive them from his home on South
England Street to the Courthouse Green or nearby lawns
where they would graze.  He was somewhat awe-inspiring,
at least to young folks, but he was friendly and after
we became acquainted with him we did not hesitate to
stop and talk to him.  He always had time to talk and
only occasionally stopped to keep his cows from running off.

4

Courtesy of Mr. Thomas Moyles

Mr. Nelson

His home was Tazewell Hall, built by John Randolph, brother of Peyton Randolph, for whom our Mr. Nelson was named. It must have been a beautiful home during its heyday but all of the time of my childhood, it was run down.

Before we moved to Main Street, when I was too young to remember, we lived on the east side of South England Street across from Tazewell Hall. My mother tells of Mr. Nelson's efforts to be a good neighbor by knocking at our door, offering pears from the trees that grew around his home.

Mr. Nelson died in Henrico County in 1955. His home was dismantled and moved to Newport News. The Williamsburg Lodge expanded over the site of Tazewell Hall. Some of the pear trees still grow there, the only reminder of "Old Man Nelson."

In many ways growing up in Williamsburg was the same as in other small towns across the country in the '30s. Life was not as hectic as it is today and things were more orderly.

I first entered school during the year of the Great Depression. Times were hard financially. As has been stated the college and Eastern State Hospital had provided employment for a good portion of Williamsburg's residents and with the rise of The Restoration in the '30s the town was in better condition than most communities of equal size. As the city was restored, tourists began to come bringing money which provided financial stability. This still exists today. My father always had a job and we were better off than many, but with five children in the family, there were few luxuries to be enjoyed. To provide these my brothers, my sister and I became very enterprising.

Besides the usual odd jobs we engaged in a variety of unusual money-making activities. We picked and sold wild flowers to the tourists. They grew in abundance in "The Bottom" during the spring and summer, especially violets. We were always on the lookout for drink bottles to return for the two cents deposit--five cents for the quart gingerale type. A small source of income which only a college town could provide came from the biology students at William and Mary. They could be seen in the Spring with insect collection nets all over town. Some of the lazier or unsuccessful students would pay kids to help them collect their quotas. Brother Clarence and I sold magazines to the male students. We went through the dorms making pests of ourselves but we managed to sell all of our magazines most of the time. Later we had paper routes and let the magazine business slide. Another source of revenue we found was selling Christmas wreaths. My father did business with a wreath factory in Charles City County and he brought home several dozen each year for us to sell. This was before the widespread use of plastic for such things. These were made of dried holly branches with plaster berries. The holly was dipped in green paint and the berries in red. Later, as teenagers we worked in stores. I worked one summer at Williamsburg Steam Laundry.

I can barely remember carnivals that were set up on Courthouse Green. There was also a small circus or two. Some people called these small traveling shows Chautauquas, from an Iroquoian Indian name meaning "Someone Was Lost Here." This was the name of a county and lake in New York. It was on the shore of the lake that an educational association was established which put on shows, the first of which opened in 1874. Around 1900 most small traveling shows of an educational nature became Chautauquas.

After the Restoration got into full swing in the early '30s the Courthouse Green was no longer available for these shows. In fact, their presentations were discouraged anywhere in the Williamsburg area. I remember very few of them in the area since the '30s.

A few things in the dim recesses of my memory are the opening of the James River bridge in 1928 and the celebration of the Sesquicentennial at Yorktown in 1931. I remember riding to Newport News and observing the fireworks set off to celebrate the opening of the bridge. What I remember about the Sesquicentennial was that Dad took Clarence and Dorothy to Yorktown to see some of the events. I had to stay home with Mom because I was stricken with diphtheria.

I remember fish peddlers blowing long odd-sounding metal horns as they drove slowly along the streets. I've read that earlier they blew conch shells and of course they drove wagons before trucks.

I remember the ice man because we kept a cardboard sign which he gave us which said "ICE" and indicated how much was needed. We hung the sign on the front door on the days the ice man came around. This announced our need for ice. It went into our icebox in the days before refrigerators.

Another childhood memory concerns smoking. When we became curious about this habit we discovered that the long seed pods of the catalpa tree could be lit and smoked. We called them "monkey cigars." I don't believe anyone ever became addicted to these as people do to tobacco but as a nonsmoker I found that "monkey cigars" tasted as good as anything made of tobacco. Some of these catalpa trees today can be found lining both sides of Palace Green.

Chapter 2


TRICKS AND TREATS


     Life was not all struggle growing up in
Williamsburg. There were many good times. We did not
have as much difficulty entertaining ourselves then as
the kids of today seem to have.

     One form of fun we had as teenaged boys was to
make what we called rubber guns. We had battles with
them in the shopping areas of Main Street.

     The gun was made with a piece of wood about a
foot long, two inches wide and one-half inch thick.
From an old inner tube we cut one-half inch wide rubber
bands, two of which were stretched around the length of
the wood. A half section of a clothes pin or similar
strong strip of wood was inserted under one end of the
tightly stretched rubber bands. A nail was driven into
the bottom of the stock a few inches from the end holding the clothes pin. When the nail, as a trigger, was
squeezed against the clothes pin, the top of the pin
would open. Into this opening was inserted another
rubber band which was looped over the opposite end of
the gun. When the trigger was squeezed, the rubber
band would fly out, a distance of 10' to 15'. We

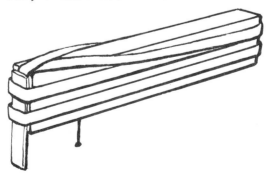

played a form of cops and robbers with these guns, taking great delight in shooting each other. Some of the guns were more elaborate than others, depending on the ingenuity of the maker. Remembering the fun we had with these guns, I tried to make one for my sons in recent years, but I found that the synthetic rubber of today's inner tubes did not have enough elasticity to work properly.

There was a game we played at night on the athletic fields of William and Mary called "Capture the Flag." Two teams were chosen with about six or eight boys on each side, one team on either end of the field. A white handkerchief or rag was placed at one end of the field, protected by one team. The team on the other side had to sneak across or around to capture the handkerchief or flag without getting tagged or tackled. Some of the members of the invading team would attempt to lure away the protectors while others would creep in and capture the flag. It was a slow game and was most successful on very dark nights, but success brought pride and joy to the winning team.

My friends and I did not always play innocent games to amuse ourselves. Sometimes we switched to pranks for amusement. Halloween, of course, was the favorite time for this type of activity. We never heard of trick or treat in those days. It was all tricks. There were such pranks as removing gates from their posts and putting garbage cans on garage roofs. There was seldom any great damage done that I ever heard of. Most of us thought two of our friends went too far when they once hoisted a dead cat up the flagpole in front of Matthew Whaley School.

The most approved prank, engaged in mainly by the younger set, was soaping up windows. This was done for the most part on the shop windows along Main Street. There was seldom a window that was not marked up with soap streaks by the end of the night. The merchants reluctantly agreed to this, feeling no doubt that it would be a release for the destructive urges of the young vandals. It only cost them a few minutes of their time next morning to wash off the soap. Occasionally, some of the meaner kids would use crayons or a candle, marks from which were harder to remove.

One trick, by some of the older boys who did not wait for Halloween, was played in the apple orchard of Judge Frank Armistead along Nassau Street. The story goes that the good judge suspected that raids were being made on a large barrel of cider which he kept in his orchard. One day he came out with sleeves rolled up to move the heavy barrel. It came up quicker than he expected since it was empty.

Another trick invented by my brother Clarence and myself was done with fine wire. My father supplemented his income by repairing radios at night. The old Atwater-Kents and Silvertones which he repaired contained small devices which yielded fine copper wire. My brother and I would stretch a length of this wire across the sidewalks up town at face level. It was practically invisible and when we caught someone across the face he could feel it but could not see it as is often the case with a cobweb. His antics of surprise and fright would send us into ill-concealed fits of laughter. We worked at hiding our tricks by pretending to scratch our heads or some such maneuver and were pretty good at it, but sometimes we were caught. Most people would be amazed at the invisible wire and end up laughing with us. We chose our victims carefully and never hurt anyone with it.

Our creative urges often led us to build tree houses or some other type of shack which we usually called a play house. Once someone gave us some large pieces of burlap which we used to build a tent. We had great fun putting this together and erecting it at various locations around our yard and in "The Bottom."

There was a time when we were teenagers that we built a log cabin. This was done on the Rockefeller estate behind Bassett Hall. We would often go to the city incinerator and sewage disposal plant at the end of South England Street. Across the street from the incinerator was the city dump which was infested with rats. We shot the rats with .22 rifles. Beyond the dump was a swamp where we often shot snakes. It was during one of these shooting expeditions that we conceived the idea of building a log cabin. On the next

trip to the area, we brought axes and hatchets and
proceeded up the hill above the dump quite a ways into
the woods.  We chopped down trees after school for
several days, building a little each day until the
cabin was at eye level.  At this point we ran out of
enthusiasm and never finished the task.  At some point
in the construction we became aware of the fact that we
were on Bassett Hall property but we felt we could
finish the job without being detected.  We revisited
the site a year or so later and the roofless cabin was
still there so we thought we had done no harm since no
one cared enough to remove the result of our labor.

     As I look back, we had more opportunities for
entertainment than most youngsters growing up in a
town the size of Williamsburg in the '30s.  The college
sponsored events such as plays, musicals, and dances.
The latter brought in the big name bands a few years
before World War II.  There were also special events
like homecoming with its parade down Main Street in
the morning, a free lunch at noon and a football game
in the afternoon.  Other athletic events such as baseball games and track and field meets could be seen in
the proper season.  A few years after the Restoration
had developed, it sponsored musical recitals, special
Christmas programs such as lighting the community tree,
dragging in the yule log and carol singing.  The
rapidly spreading fame of the little restored city
brought in famous people from all walks of life.

     In 1940, Williamsburg was the setting for a
full length motion picture "The Howards of Virginia."

Many of the scenes were shot on the streets of the
restored area and nearby Carter's Grove. Some of my
classmates from Matthew Whaley were hired as extras
in the movie which starred Cary Grant and Martha Scott.
I was content to join friends in chasing Cary Grant
around. We caught up with him once on the campus of
William and Mary. To see him close we had to chase
him since he moved around quickly from place to place.

Another famous visitor from the movie world
was Shirley Temple. She arrived with her parents in
the early forties. I caught a glimpse of her leaving
the Williamsburg Inn where she was lodged. Since those
days Williamsburg has seen so many national and international figures that its people have become somewhat
blasé. The famous visitors have included actors,
writers, artists, kings and other world leaders as
**well as most of our own presidents.**

Corner of Francis and Nassau Streets. Eastern State House on left. First Baptist Church
and Persons's Garage. Cole House on right.

Chapter 3

MATTHEW WHALEY SCHOOL

As stated earlier, everyone in Williamsburg knew
everyone else during the '30s. I believe I knew at least
90 percent of the people. Families moved into town a
few at a time and this made it easy to become acquainted
with them, especially if they had school-aged children.
Of course, everyone in Matthew Whaley knew everyone else,
except perhaps the children of the first few grades.
Matthew Whaley School contained all eleven grades until
1947 when a twelfth grade was added. The twelfth grade
was added to Bruton Heights School in 1950. James Blair
High School was completed in 1955 at Casey's Corner to
provide space for increased enrollment. Since then
several other schools have been built to keep up with
the rapidly expanding population.

As in the case with most students, school took
more of my time than any other single activity.
Consequently, teachers and classmates were the largest
group of people affecting my life during the years of
this narrative.

There is little that I can remember about the
first few grades. The first grade in the old school
is remembered for two things--learning the alphabet and
a mischievous classmate. The alphabet was posted as a
frieze along the top of the blackboard. The letters,
in a beautiful script, were printed white on a black
background. The boy sitting in one corner of the classroom was Jess Jackson. His constant smile and somewhat
roguish nature attracted me to him and we began a
friendship which continues to this day. The teacher
was Miss Mary Acree.

The first grade in the new school was taught

Matthew Whaley School — 1929

by Miss Williams, second grade by Miss Mary Acree and third grade by Miss Powell. Miss Jeanne Etheridge, who later became principal, taught the fourth grade.

The school activity which I enjoyed most was art and since I seemed to have some talent in this subject the teachers kept me busy from the start with drawing and painting. It was in the fifth grade, taught by Miss Maxie Acree, that I was occupied the whole year working on art projects. I spent most of the year on my knees, drawing scenes from our studies of ancient Egypt, Greece, and Rome as well as the Middle Ages. The paintings were done on large rolls of paper which were hung or stuck on the walls around the classroom. With me on these projects were two of my good friends, Irvin Douglas and Bat Peachy.

Sixth grade was taught by Miss Myrtle Cooper, a likable lady who had such a knack for teaching that she made learning an enjoyable experience for everyone. I continued to improve my grades by illustrating the projects. This I was able to do, at least to some extent, through the ninth grade.

Beginning at the seventh grade we changed classes and had different teachers for each subject. Miss Eunice Hall stands out in my memory for teaching social studies with a no-nonsense approach. She was somewhat strict but it was Miss Ida Trosvig who held the title of Number One in strictness. She inspired awe in most students and there was an air of quiet study in her ninth grade classes. For mathematics in the seventh and eighth grades, I believe, there was Mary Scott Howison, a sweet and patient lady who taught me most of the little bit of math I was able to absorb.

After her was George C. Pitts who taught math and gym and went on to become principal. Mildred Matier taught English and was active in all the dramatic pre-sentations. She directed most of the plays and pageants.

The art teacher was Miss Mary Wall Christian, a dedicated and popular member of the school faculty. She encouraged my interest in art and helped me to look to it for my future career. She also acted as a substitute teacher for some of the lower grades.

Music classes were taught by Miss Harriet Bozarth. Her family was prominent in several business ventures around town. I took a boys home economics class taught by Miss Marshall. The basics of sewing and cooking she taught were to be very useful in future years. Shop teachers didn't stay as long as the other teachers. The only one I can recall is Mr. Everett Teal. In shop I learned how to do some woodwork, part of it on a lathe. My most successful project was a pair of book ends with a cut-out dog, front end on one side and tail end on the other side.

One of my extra-curricular activities was writing. I joined a classmate, James Bailey, in writing a nature column for the school paper "The Powder Horn." When baseball season came in, James went out for it and I continued to write the column alone.

Another activity I enjoyed was singing in the Glee Club. We sang such stirring songs as "Give Me Some Stout-Hearted Men" and "Juanita" as well as the songs of Stephen Foster. I had learned to appreciate music in the sixth grade when Miss Cooper played recordings of Walter Damrosch.

Others I remember from Matthew Whaley were Mrs. Myra Gregory who worked in the office and Mr. C. C. Briggs who conducted the band. Two members of the college Department of Education were supervisors of instruction. They were Dr. Inga Helseth and Dr. Helen Weeks. In addition to their duties as mentioned above, they were responsible for directing William and Mary students in practice teaching.

Courtesy of *Daily Press*

Miss Jeanne Etheridge

Courtesy of Mr. Jack Goodwin

Miss Mary Wall Christian

Most of my school days were spent in classes where student teachers were present to learn how to handle a class while helping our teachers. I thought that all schools had student teachers. It was years later that I learned that Matthew Whaley was a model school, under the guidance of William and Mary from its earliest days. The history of Matthew Whaley has been well documented in other publications so we need only say here that William and Mary had maintained a school for needy children for many years. It was in 1894 that the college opened the first Model and Practice School. When the new school opened in 1930, it was with funds and guidance from William and Mary for the purpose of using it for the teacher training program of the college. This was obviously equally beneficial to the school, the college, teachers and students.

16

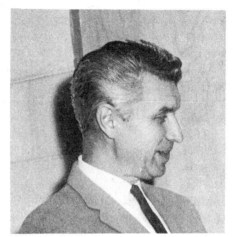

Courtesy of Daily Press                    Courtesy of Daily Press

Mr. Rawls Byrd                              Mr. George Pitts

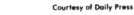

At the head of this unique educational plant
was a man who was to be prominent in educational
circles in Williamsburg for almost forty years.  He
was Rawls Byrd, a William and Mary graduate who became
superintendent of Williamsburg's schools in 1928.  This
included only Williamsburg High School and the Matty
School at first, then the combined grammar and high school
when the new Matthew Whaley was opened in 1930.  A
mild-mannered man, he was seldom if ever known to show
anger.  He handled problems of discipline in a firm but
fair manner.  He was certainly an able administrator.
His responsibility increased when Bruton Heights opened
in 1940 and again in 1955 when James Blair High School
emerged.  Mr. Byrd was successful in his efforts to have
the school systems of Williamsburg and James City County
combined in 1953.  He retired in 1964, but was honored
in 1965 by having an elementary school named for him.
He died in 1979, but will long be remembered for his
contributions to education in Williamsburg.

A few words must be written here about a man
who had a leading part in planning the organization of
Matthew Whaley before it opened.  He was Dr. Kremer J.
Hoke, who was head of the Department of Education and
Dean of the college.  We were reminded of his contri-
butions to our school by a large portrait of him which

hung at the entrance to the school auditorium. Dr. Hoke first came to William and Mary in 1920 as head of the Summer school. Organizations in which he held membership were the National Society of College Teachers and Phi Beta Kappa among many others. He wrote two books and found time to work on the program of instruction at the State Penitentiary.

# THE POWDER HORN

Subscription Price - 50c Per Year —— Single Copies - 10c

**Published Monthly By the Pupils of**

## MATTHEW WHALEY HIGH SCHOOL

Member of
Columbia Scholastic
Press Association

Member of
Southern
Interscholastic Press
Association

### EDITORIAL STAFF

CO-EDITORS ........................................ Rupert Noble and Guy White
Senior Editor ................................................................. Madison Wright
Associate Editor ................................................................ Preston Cocke

**Assistant Editors:** Ione Faison, Mary B. Henderson, Helen Woods, William Snyder, Marjorie Karlson, James Prosoco, Buddy Geddy, Doris Parker, M. H. Hines, E. M. Baker, Thornton Slater, Catherine Jones.

**Reporters:** M. McGinnis, Frances Robb, Frances Brigham, Nancy Bozarth, Dorothy Belvin, Bobby Voyles, Alan Taylor.

### BUSINESS STAFF

CO-BUSINESS MANAGERS ................ Charles Renick, Jane Brigham
ASSISTANT BUSINESS MANAGERS:
Jewel Kidd, Norman Hornsby, Buddy Geddy, B. Brigham.
FACULTY ADVISOR .................................................. Wm. H. Kendrick

Masthead School Newspaper--1941

Any proper account of Matthew Whaley in the '30s must include mention of the custodian, Mr. Frank Sawyer. Most of the older boys called him Tom. Many of us thought that was his name. I believe most of us would have said that he was the janitor if someone asked us,

18

"Tom" Sawyer

Courtesy of Mrs. B.E. Bishop

but he was more than that. He was a maintenance man,
disciplinarian, and someone who would lend a sympathe-
tic ear to anyone's problems. He could fix anything
from a broken toilet seat to a broken friendship. He
became a father figure to many of the students who
could always count on his help in times of difficulty.
He was anything but soft spoken, however. We often
heard him yell down the hall, "What are you boys doing
there?" Any mischief was dealt with firmly by Mr.
Sawyer. He could straighten out most problems of
discipline but if not, he didn't hesitate to inform
Mr. Byrd about the offending student.

Mr. Sawyer sometimes incurred the wrath of
some teachers through his language. A log cabin was
built on the elementary side of the school to give
the students an impression of frontier life. Once when
Sawyer discovered boys climbing on its roof he was
heard to yell, "Get the hell off of there." Another
time when "Tom" overstepped the bounds of his position was when he walked into an elementary class and
found the tables and chairs pushed back helter-
skelter from the center of the room. The pupils
were gathered in a group seated on the floor. He
said something such as, "What the devil are you kids
doing with the furniture like that?" He didn't see
the teacher at first but she soon made her presence
known to him and promptly put him in his place with
these words. "MR. SAWYER, I'm in charge of this
class and I'll be responsible for the children and
the furniture."

In spite of a few instances such as these, Frank Sawyer did a remarkable job of maintaining a school the size of Matthew Whaley. He did it alone at first but later had an assistant who mainly looked after the furnaces. The school was an important part of Sawyer's life and he seemed determined to see that it was properly cared for. Those of us who were associated with the school in any way in those days will never forget him.

In those days, playing marbles was a popular pastime among boys. When we were in the lower grades, we played at every opportunity. We played for keeps and the best player collected most of the available marbles. Money was scarce and if anyone lost all his marbles, he had to wait until more money was acquired to buy more marbles. The larger ones, about an inch in diameter, we called "shooters." Hollow metal balls we called "hollies" and solid ball bearings were called "steelies." They were all traded among us like gems of different values. The unusual colored glass marbles were more rare and thus could be traded for several of the more common types.

In early spring the elementary grades planted a garden. Only fast growing things like radishes and lettuce were planted so they could be harvested before school closed in June.

The extra-curricular activity in which I participated for more years than any other was scouting. I joined the Boy Scouts when I was in the eighth grade and remained with them until graduation four years later.

At first the scoutmaster was Rutherfoord Goodwin but later George Pitts, our math teacher and gym coach, took the position. Pitts later became principal of James Blair High School. Most of the time the scout meetings were held in the school gymnasium where we had ample space to carry on the activities of scouting. Before my school and scouting careers closed we began to meet in the Methodist Church on the corner of Main and Boundary streets. The war in Europe had begun to intrude upon our peaceful existence and as scouts we took turns watching for planes from the church tower.

I had a fondness for all scouting activities, but most of all I enjoyed hiking and camping. There

were camping trips along the newly completed Parkway to
Yorktown in the late '30s and a Jamboree on the beach
that I recall. We camped with other troops from throughout the Peninsula. One camping trip I remember in particular. Our camp was on the site of the Confederate fort
at Jones Mill Pond along the Parkway and the highlight
of the trip was the discovery of ammunition known as
"Minnie Balls." The few I found I kept for many years
afterward.

The fellowship and joy of outdoor activity made
scouting an important part of my youth and will always
be remembered with fondness.

I graduated from Matthew Whaley in 1941 and was
beset by the feelings of nostalgia common in those days
to most people who spent all their school years in one
building. However, I don't believe I fully appreciated
the uniqueness of the school or the town at that time.
Somewhat responsible for this lack was the constant
press of school work, after school employment, and other
activities. In addition, we could see the steadily
increasing threat of the war situation.

By the time of graduation, I had decided to
attend William and Mary to further my education. With
the threat of U.S. involvement in the war the economy
began to improve. As soon as I became sixteen, the
legal age to hold a regular job, I worked after school
and on Saturdays. I felt that I could put myself through
college by living at home and working. My parents were
not able to finance college for me so I knew it was up
to me to do so.

As stated earlier, I had become involved in some
kind of enterprise for most of my childhood. I looked
forward to the time I could work full time and become
at least somewhat independent, financially. My first
regular job was at the Williamsburg Steam Laundry. I
worked there the first summer in which I became sixteen.
The work was hard and hot and the pay was low but I
learned a good deal and made some good friends.

Soon after I went back to school that fall, I
found employment at the A & P store, uptown. This was
an interesting job where I met a good portion of
Williamsburg's citizens. I worked with several schoolmates and we enjoyed ourselves while competing for the

good graces of the Manager, Gerald Bracey.

I was employed at the A & P through graduation and my entrance at William and Mary in the fall of 1941. The "Day of Infamy" at Pearl Harbor was only three months away at this time and was to change my life as it did the lives of most people living at that time.

Courtesy of Mr. James Bowry

School Group on Courthouse Green — 1920s

Williamsburg High School coming down, Palace going up.

Author's Family Photo

Brother Clarence's class around 1940. Clarence with elbow above Jeff Carter, lying prone. Jack Goodwin standing on left with his mother.

Chapter 4

GROWING PAINS AND PLEASURES

We were an average family, as far as I can determine.  My parents were hard-working and this was one of
their characteristics passed on to all five of their
children to some extent.  Mother must be named as the
hardest working member of the group.  Although Dad put
in his eight to ten hours as necessary at that time and
repaired whatever needed repair, when his day's work was
done he sat down to read the daily newspaper and expected
Mom and the kids to do the rest.  It was Mom who arose
early in the morning to make the fires to warm up the
house.  We first had wood stoves and later switched to
coal.  The house was two-storied and had two chimneys
with an opening in each room, as many houses were built
in those days.  Although there was the usual bickering
to be expected in a family of five children, we were
taught to look after each other.  We did this, at least
to some extent, as shown by an event which occurred
when I was about thirteen.

My brother, Clarence, and I would often go on
pecan gathering expeditions since there were several
trees near home.  There were two of these trees growing
along the brick wall at the Courthouse, built in 1932
at the corner of Francis and South England Streets.
We climbed one of these to knock down pecans.  I
reached for a limb which came off in my hand.  I remember a downward plunge and then nothing.  I had been
knocked unconscious by landing on the brick sidewalk
which ran parallel to the wall around the courthouse.
When I awoke, I was being dragged homeward by Clarence.
He helped me upstairs to the bathroom and washed me
off to the best of his ability.  With Mom's considerable

energy went a high degree of excitability which we both
tried to avoid activating, but it was no use. I was
wounded and pale. When Mom saw me she acted as expected
and promptly hustled me off to the doctor. However,
my injuries required only three stitches--one above the
right eye, one on the right knee and one on the left
elbow. It was not much treatment needed for one who had
fallen about fifteen feet and had landed on a brick
sidewalk.

I was born in Gloucester County, about twenty
miles from Williamsburg. My ancestors lived there and
in York County since the middle of the seventeenth
century. I was two when my parents moved to Williamsburg.
Clarence was only a few months old. My sister, Dorothy,
and my brothers, Billy and Bobby, were born in the little
colonial city.

We visited relatives in Gloucester and they came
over to see us. Two of my uncles, my father's youngest
brother and my mother's only brother, stayed with us for
a while at different times. They came over to seek
employment during the depression. The memory of my
mother's brother, James Rowe, remains vividly in mind
because he was difficult to awaken. The task of waking
him each morning fell to Clarence and me. We tried
yelling, shaking, and even dumping his bed. We usually
succeeded, but only with extreme effort. Finally, we
found a quick way to solve the problem. Mom kept
smelling salts in the house. One whiff of this power-
ful smelling substance and Uncle James came up fighting
for air, wide awake. Everyone had a good laugh at the
way we solved the problem, even James, who was a good-
natured soul.

Behind the house at 209 Francis Street was a
shed in which we kept coal. Against this shed Clarence
and I built a lean-to shack where we played, worked on
school projects and kept kindling wood. One time, we
decided to install a light in the shed. We acquired an
old lamp and a bunch of discarded wiring from different
sources. The wire was varied in thickness and type but
we thought wire was wire and that electricity would flow
through all of it. We spliced all the pieces together
with the lamp on one end and a plug on the other. It

was about twenty-five feet in length. We plugged it
into the house current and fire flew throughout the
length of the wire. We only burned out a fuse but we
learned a lesson about electricity which we never
forgot.

In the wood shed were born several generations
of kittens. We were all fond of animals and we allowed
the cats to proliferate. At one time we had about two
dozen. One of them, named Mary, had a litter in the
hollow branch of a large tree at the corner of Nassau
and Francis Streets. We had several dogs during this
time; the most memorable being a small male rat-terrier
we called "Spot." We kept him several years before he
disappeared.

Billy once had a rabbit which he cared for
devotedly for a few weeks. Then, he wearied of the task
and Mom was left to feed it. Not wanting to see any
creature in our care starve, she fed the rabbit for
a while and finally gave it away. About three days later,
she asked Billy, "When did you last feed the rabbit?"
He answered, "Don't worry Mom, I fed him this morning."
"That's funny," she replied. "I gave it away three
days ago." Billy said no more.

We were a pretty close family. Most of our
recreation together was enjoyed on weekends. Dad's
favorite pastime was fishing and he often required
Clarence and me to go with him, which we did, sometimes reluctantly. However, if the fish were biting,
we were happy to be along. Our best fishing spot was
on the Navy's fuel oil pier at Yorktown. Dad was a
friend of Bennie Bray who was in charge of the pier
and we had an open invitation to fish there. A plat-
form was built under the pier, close to the water,
which provided shade on hot days. It was pleasant to
fish from this area and the spot and croaker were
usually plentiful. Most of the time we brought home
a dozen or two including flounder and pigfish, which
we called "hogfish." We always threw back or killed
the ugly toadfish, eels, and small sharks called
"dogfish."

Sometimes we rented a rowboat to go out to
York Spit Lighthouse or up to the Naval Mine Depot

vicinity. Dad always kept a small outboard motor
which he could attach to a rented boat. The boats were
rented by the DeNeufville family (pronounced locally
as Donnervul). They lived in a cottage on the beach
and rented boats for many years. They were descended
from a French Huguenot family who migrated to Virginia
before the Revolution. The National Park Service
bought the cottage in recent years and restored it as
the "Archer Cottage" of colonial times.

Other good times at Yorktown included picnics
enjoyed by the whole family. We would often meet
relatives there who would come from Newport News.
We swam, played ball and explored the marl cliffs
from noon 'til dark on summer Sundays.

Once Dad bought a sailboat which he didn't
keep very long. He anchored it with Mr. DeNeufville's
boats and he kept an eye on it for Dad. One day Dad
and two of his friends, Clyde Robins and Pete Hunt,
went fishing in the sailboat. Clarence went with them
and they caught quite a few fish in spite of the windy
weather. They had their hands full with sailing and
fishing, but they managed all right until they were
coming to shore. When they were only a few yards from
the beach, a sudden gust of wind swung the boom around
and caught them by surprise. They all pitched over on
one side to avoid the boom and the boat capsized. Well,
the water was only up to their waists so they righted
the boat and managed to salvage all the fishing gear and
other supplies. They were somewhat upset with Clarence,
however, since all he was worried about salvaging was
the soft drinks.

Soon after this experience Dad decided that sailing was not his sport, so he sold the boat.

Mom encouraged us to go to Sunday School as soon as we were old enough to walk there alone. We became Baptists, because Mom was Baptist. Dad was Methodist, but not very devout at that time. We attended Williamsburg Baptist Church which was on Main Street near the Powder Horn. (It was later called Powder Magazine, as in Colonial times.) The church moved to a new building on Richmond Road in 1934. The Restoration helped finance this move to make way for restoring the colonial area.

Courtesy of Dr. Carlton Casey

Williamsburg Baptist Church before 1934

A typical Sunday morning, in warm weather, was spent on the front porch swing, watching the ladies across the fence at the Asylum. From around the corner would come the sounds of hymns, sung by the colored folks of the First Baptist Church on Nassau Street. It was located in the middle of the block, next to where

Person's garage was before it burned. We didn't know it then or care, but this church was built in 1855. Often, we could hear the preacher when he raised his voice to make a point. Then we could hear the congregation respond with "Amen." We could hear better in warm weather through the open windows. There was no air-conditioning in town then.

Sometimes we cranked up the old record player, which we called a Victoria, and listened to a few scratchy records. "My Blue Heaven" was the first popular song I can remember, to which I paid any attention. We listened to the radio and heard "Amos & Andy," "Lum & Abner," "Fibber McGee & Molly," "Fred Allen," "Jack Benny" and "The Shadow" in the evening.

When we had whiled away the morning Mom would call us in to lunch, which we called "dinner." The evening meal was "supper." When we finished all the fried chicken, collard greens, sweet potatoes, corn bread and iced tea, we would lie around reading comic books or the Sunday funnies. Sometimes we would all pile into the car and ride to Gloucester to see our grandparents, uncles, aunts and cousins. We didn't like to wait for the ferry at Yorktown but we enjoyed the ride when it came.

When we first moved to Francis Street, we were young enough to enjoy playing hide-and-seek, giant steps, marbles and mumblety-peg with the

Author's Family Photo

209 Francis Street with Brother's friend

neighbors. As we grew older, we practiced various
crafts such as pottery, drawing and model making.
Drawing was my favorite hobby but I also enjoyed
making model airplanes. As the thirties gave way to
the forties and the clouds of war began to threaten,
building model planes became increasingly popular.
Flying-model and solid-model kits were both available
at the local Five and Dime Store. Solid-models were
made by carving the fusilage, wings, and tail assembly
from a solid block of balsa wood. It was then sanded
to a smooth finish, painted and the insignia were
glued on with great care. Decals had not been very

well-developed at this time. The flying models were made
by gluing balsa strips together to form the body, wings,
etc. This frame was covered by a layer of thin paper. A
rubber band was hooked inside the tail and led to the
propeller, which was twisted, winding up the rubber band.
When released, the plane sailed off for a short way.
As in the real world of aviation, there were a lot of
crash landings.

I enjoyed reading and did as much of it as
possible as a teenager. The municipal library was con-
veniently located down the street from home at the
courthouse. Miss Ann Chapman was the librarian and was
greatly loved by all. She guarded such treasures as
Mark Twain's stories of Tom Sawyer and Huckleberry Finn.
It was here that I became familiar with the writings of
Jack London, Earnest Seton Thompson and Edgar Rice
Burroughs. Mrs. Fannie Clark Nightengale worked at the
library and checked out the books for me.

As we grew older, we explored our world in ever-
widening circles around home, as most youngsters do every-
where. After tiring of the joys to be found in the Bottom
we familiarized ourselves with the Uptown area, only about

two blocks from home. Several of our school mates lived
in the vicinity of South England Street and this became a
favorite hangout. Eventually we pushed on beyond the
houses to the dump and swamp as described earlier.

The college was a fine place to explore. We
became familiar with most of the buildings on the campus.
Sometimes there were demonstrations in physics and chemistry that we could watch. Once Clarence and I were
shown around the biology building, Washington Hall, by a
young professor or graduate student. We were greatly
impressed, especially by a human fetus bottled in for-
maldehyde. There were also some Rhesus monkeys caged in
a greenhouse on the south side of Washington Hall. We
were told that they were used in experiments but no
details were given.

Beyond the college was Lake Matoaka and the
nature trails in the surrounding woods. We swam in the
lake in summer and skated on it in winter. In the
'30s, the winters were colder than in recent years and
we quite often had an opportunity to get out on the ice.
A few people had ice skates then but most of the kids slid
around in their shoes. I once tried to ride a bicycle on
the ice of Matoaka with near disastrous results when the
wheels went out from under me. Once was enough of that.

In the woods between the college and the lake was
a CCC camp. This was a part of President Roosevelt's New
Deal, established soon after he was inaugurated in 1933. We
had studied about his administration in school and we knew
something about the CCC, WPA, PWA, NRA, etc. We learned
that the New Deal was Roosevelt's plan to help the country
recover from The Depression. In 1933, this CCC camp began
construction of Matoaka Park with the aid of the National
Park Service. This was an extensive project in which 1,200
acres of woodland was to be developed and converted into a
scenic park. This acreage was bought for the college by
J. A. C. Chandler in 1919 with a park in mind, but no work
was begun until 1933. It was dedicated in October 1934 in
a program which coincided with the inauguration of John
Stewart Bryan as president of the college. He succeeded
Chandler who died May 31 of that year. The park included
trails which began and ended at the lily pond on Campus
Road. They criss-crossed the park for several miles

Courtesy of William & Mary Library

Matoaka Boathouse

leading to the lake shore.  Rustic wooden bridges were
built over several of the streams feeding the lake.  A
bridle path led for six miles within the park and a boathouse was built on the lake, housing rowboats and canoes
for recreation and instruction of William & Mary students.
  An important feature of the park was an outdoor
amphitheater called "Player's Dell" constructed in a natural
hollow.  The seats were made from split chestnut logs.  The
college had long wanted a natural setting for plays, concerts,
etc.  I watched much of the construction of Matoaka Park,
roaming the trails, swimming in the lake and occasionally
using the boats and canoes at the boathouse.  Today the campus
has expanded, covering the area that was Matoaka Park and
little trace of it remains.

Chapter 5

THE PEOPLE OF WILLIAMSBURG

Many of the people of Williamsburg influenced the life of this writer as he grew to manhood in the little city. In addition to family, classmates and teachers, there were friends, neighbors, employers and scout leaders.

The first neighbors I remember were the Baker family. They moved next door to us when we moved to the house on Francis Street. There were three girls and a boy. A few years after we moved there another boy and a girl were born, so it was a fairly large family. They seemed to be happy and we remained on friendly terms with them. Mr. Baker worked as a carpenter for the Restoration. He was an outgoing person who would yell when he came home from work to let his family know that he was home. One of his younger daughters was named Edna Mae but he called her "Bullet". Sometimes he would add "Buckshot, Cannonball" to her name.

Author's Family Photo

"Bullet" with author

Mr. Baker died soon after his youngest daughter was born and his family moved to York Street. After this, the family could not remain together so they were separated. Mrs. Baker remarried and moved out of town. Only the elder son remained in Williamsburg.

When the Bakers moved from beside us on Francis Street, Mr. and Mrs. Clyde Johnson moved in. He worked for the college power plant. He once conducted brother Clarence and myself through the plant and I remember being awed by the huge dynamos humming loudly in the dimly lit building. The smell of oil was quite strong and the total effect left a lasting impression on me. The Johnsons had a son, born soon after they moved next to us.

The third and last family to live beside us on Francis street was the A.T. Vaughn family. This also was a large family, with five girls and a boy. Mr. Vaughan worked as a bricklayer for the Restoration. My family didn't seem to be compatible with this group and with seven of us and eight of them, there was quite a bit of feuding and fussing. This faded away however, as we grew older. They remained beside us until we moved in 1950.

Among those well-remembered in my childhood were several doctors and dentists. Our first family doctor was David J. King. He was greatly loved by all whom he served and he had a special skill with children. He received my attention and affection by drawing cartoons and funny doodles on his prescription pad while visiting me when I was sick. This was at home, since most doctors made house calls in those days. Dr. King was the college physician, a part-time position until recent years. In 1930, a medical facility was built, called The College Hospital, which cost $75,000. When Dr. King died in 1935, the name of the facility was changed to "The David J. King Infirmary" in his honor.

After Dr. King's death our family doctor was J. Randolph Tucker, another dedicated man. He not only made house calls but came in all kinds of weather and when he was sick himself. He served us until he was forced to retire through illness in the early '60's.

Other doctors remembered were Brantley Henderson who was an eye, ear, nose and throat specialist and Henry Davis. After a few years as a dentist and more as a general practitioner around town, Dr. Davis limited his practice to Eastern State Hospital. His son, Hiram became Virginia's Commissioner of Mental Hygiene.

No account of medical practice in Williamsburg would be complete without mention of Dr. Baxter I. Bell, Sr. This most dedicated of all doctors established the first hospital in town in 1930. A native of Swan Quarter, North Carolina, he graduated from the Medical College of Virginia in 1915. After his internship, he came to Williamsburg and set up a clinic in the old Williamsburg Hotel, near the Powder Horn. He helped Dr. King serve the college and became its only physician when Dr. King died. He could be seen at any hour of day or night making house calls all over the Williamsburg area. He died in 1963 and is buried near his friend and associate in medicine, Dr. Tucker, in Cedar Grove Cemetery. His son, Dr. Baxter Bell, Jr. practices in Williamsburg today.

Among the dentists I recall was Dr. W.L.L. Smoot, who practiced in the '20's and '30's. He was on the school board from 1924 to 1933. His daughter lives in the area today. Dr. L.V. Henderson, brother of Brantley Henderson, practiced dentistry in the '30's.

Williamsburg's most well-known dentist was Dr. Henry M. Stryker. His fame came from his long-time service as Mayor. He served in this capacity from 1948 to 1968, longer than any of the previous mayors. He was affectionately known as "Polly" to his friends. He grew up in Williamsburg and saw all the changes take place before and after the restoration. He was fond of telling of his youth in Williamsburg and could sometimes be persuaded to tell tales on the many renowned visitors from around the world, whom he greeted as long-time mayor. My first dental work was done by Dr. Stryker and he is remembered for his quiet, gentle treatment.

Among other people I recall in those early years on Francis Street was Mr. R.H. Gilliam who lived on the outskirts of town in James City County. My mother

34

Courtesy of Daily Press

Billy Person

Courtesy of Mrs. Kitty Underwood

Justice Dick Gilliam

bought buttermilk from him, which he delivered once
a week in his Model T Ford.  He was a kind gentleman
who sometimes gave us the benefit of his homespun
philosophy.  He was a 'Police Justice', hearing traffic
and minor cases, in somewhat the manner of a judge.

Once he almost wrecked his Model T because of
my sister, Dorothy.  We were playing marbles on Main
Street in front of Mr. C.B Griffin's store.  One of
us accidently shot a marble into the street and
Dorothy ran after it.  Mr. Gilliam happened along in
his car and ran up on the median to avoid hitting my
sister.  It was before the street was made into a
single lane.  There was no harm done except to Mr.
Gilliam's dignity and possibly to his nerves.

We were acquainted with other members of his
family.  Two of his sons still live in the Williamsburg
area today and at least two of his grandsons still live
here.  One of his daughters lives in Yorktown. They believe they descend from Huguenots who settled around
Richmond in the colonial era (probably at Manakintowne).

Another well-remembered gentleman from those
days was Mr. Thomas L. Thomas, who delivered our mail
for many years.  His son, Dwight was in my class at
school and we were good friends.  Mr. Thomas lived near
the village of Magruder, which was taken over by Camp
Peary in later years.  This was in York County and he
was to take interest in its politics, serving at the
polling places after he retired from the Post Office.

Soon after my family moved to Francis Street in 1930, we observed a fire one night. It was around the corner from us on Nassau Street at Person Motor Corp. The garage was completely destroyed. The fire was started by a visiting representative from the Ford Motor Co. It seems that he was attempting to clean up deposits of oil and dirt from the garage floor by softening it with gasoline. When he scraped it with a metal scraper, sparks flew and fire resulted. The Ford Company's insurance paid for the damage.

The business was started by Charles Person in 1908. It was the first Ford dealership in Virginia. In 1925 the business was taken over by Charles's son, William Lundsford Person (Billy to his friends). The elder Person died in 1928. The family lived on the corner of Nassau and Main Streets. The property was sold to Dr. Goodwin December 24, 1927 and he transferred it to Williamsburg Holding Corporation January 3, 1928. This was the forerunner of Colonial Williamsburg. The Persons rented the property from the Corporation until 1930. Then a new building was built on the corner of Boundary and Francis Streets for the dealership. A new home was built on Richmond Road.

Billy had grown up around cars. He became involved in the business at an early age, traveling to Detroit with his brothers to bring back cars to sell. He drove "taxi" for his father for a while. He was raised as one of six children in a close family. Billy died in 1980.

His sister, Alice, is the only surviving one of the six children. She entered William and Mary in 1918, being one of the first coeds admitted after the college changed its all male policy in that year.

She taught at the Matty School until 1925. From that
time until recent years, she kept books for her father
and brother.

Billy was graduated from William and Mary in 1924
with a degree in business and was active in alumni
activities and served on its board of directors. He
was also on the board of directors of the Athletic
Educational Foundation. His activities in business
and community affairs were quite numerous.

Everyone familiar with Williamsburg has heard
or read about the way the city was restored. It has
often been repeated about Dr. W.A.R. Goodwin coming
to Bruton Parish Church as its rector in the early years
of this century. He became greatly interested in the
old buildings and the history surrounding them. He left
Williamsburg for a ministry in Rochester, N.Y. in
1909, returning as rector in 1926. In 1924 he spoke to
the Phi Beta Kappa Society in New York City about
Williamsburg and the college. John D. Rockefeller, Jr.
was in the audience and became interested in Dr.
Goodwin's plan of restoring the little city. He visited
Williamsburg in 1926 and a year lated decided to ful-
fill Dr. Goodwin's dream. Thus, another important part
of the city's history began.

Dr. Goodwin remarried after the death of his first
wife by whom he had five children. One of these was
Rutherfoord who became head of the Historical Research
Department of the Williamsburg Restoration.

Courtesy of Daily Press

Dr. Goodwin                    Mr. Rockefeller

Dr. Goodwin had three sons by his second wife, Ethel. The youngest, Jack, was a classmate and is a close friend of this writer. From Jack I heard stories of the relationship between the Goodwins and the Rockefellers.

Although Mr. Rockefeller was a Baptist, he would sometimes attend the worship services of the other churches in Williamsburg. I remember his attendance at Williamsburg Baptist after it was built on Richmond Road. He would arrive in an aging but well-kept and highly-polished Buick, chauffeur driven and enter as inconspicuously as possible. The congregation showed remarkable restraint by paying little attention to him.

There was a man well-known in Williamsburg who did not live here. He lived in Toano but Williamsburg was part of his territory and he was often seen in and around town. He was the area game warden, the first one assigned to the local area by the Commonwealth of Virginia. I remember him during the 1930s and 1940s. He had the additional title of Special Officer which enabled him to help the sheriffs, especially in operations such as spotting and destroying stills.

No man was ever more appropriately named than was Lightfoot Richardson, Game Warden and Special Officer. He had an uncanny ability to catch people breaking the fishing and game laws. No spot in the countries surrounding Williamsburg was too remote to escape his

unending surveillance. Often when I was fishing with my
dad in the fresh water ponds and lakes, Lightfoot would
pop out from the woods near us. He would check to see
if our fishing licenses were in order.

Hunters were as apt to be caught in any illegal
activity as fishermen. It was common knowledge that
Mr. Richardson would spend all night if necessary,
stalking hunters to catch them killing game at night.
His dedication to duty was responsible for the oft
repeated statement that he would arrest his own mother
if he caught her breaking the law. Apparently, he
never had that opportunity but he was known to have
arrested his own son for illegal hunting.

Chapter 6

OLD TIME BUSINESS

Before Duke of Gloucester or Main Street was restored to its colonial appearance in the early '30s, business was conducted in stores and shops from one end of it to the other. The old courthouse (of 1770) marked the dividing line between "Uptown" and "Downtown." Uptown for the most part was from the courthouse to College Corner and Downtown began at the courthouse and went to the Capitol. Some people, however, considered anything west of the courthouse to be Uptown and everything east of it to be Downtown.

Courtesy of Daily Press

Downtown

Since Judge Frank Armistead's house and Bruton
Parish Church and graveyard took up the length of
one block and the Old Courthouse and Courthouse Green
took most of another, all on the north side, it is
safe enough to say that most of the business establish-
ments were on the south side of Main Street. Dwelling
houses were scattered among the places of business
throughout the length of the street and some shop
keepers lived upstairs over their stores.

Old Courthouse being restored

After the street was restored, most of the
businesses were moved in the block adjacent to the
college now known as Merchant's Square. The Restoration built a colonial style building on the north
side of the street near the capitol and rented it to
the A&P Tea Co. This became the "Down-town A&P."
Diagonally across the street on the southeast corner
of Botetourt Street the same thing was done for
Penders. This was the food store chain which later
became Colonial Stores and today is Big Star. Of
course, there was an Up-town A&P and an Up-town
Penders. The down-town stores were built to appease
some influential ladies who lived downtown and

objected to walking uptown to shop—or so the story
goes. In those days few families had more than one
car and not many women drove. The Down-town A&P store
was managed for a while by an uncle of mine. There
was not enough trade to support the store so the
company closed it and Uncle Lester moved to Newport
News and found employment in the shipyard.

Soon after this, a drug store was opened in
the building and managed by Clarence Hall. He was
a brother of Clyde and Thad Hall who operated the
Rexall Drug Store uptown. We called his store "The
Down-town Rexall" or "Rexall No. Two." After World
War II, when "Doc Hall" retired, the Restoration
converted the building to its original function of
colonial times and today it is called "Water's
Storehouse."
The Down-town Penders was managed for a while by
Russell Wing. When it closed, Mr. Wing opened
his own store on the corner of Page Street and
Penniman Road.

**Uptown — 1932**

Among the businesses in town in the '30's,
were several Greek owned restaurants. One of the
most popular was The Capitol Restaurant, owned and
operated by Angelo Costas, his wife, Dora, and Tom
Baltas, and his wife, Helen.

Angelo and Tom left Greece together in 1914.
Tom went to Pennsylvania and Angelo went to Norfolk.
In 1916, Angelo arrived in Williamsburg with his
brother Nick and two friends. They opened the town's
first restaurant, The Norfolk Cafe, downtown across
the street from The Paradise House. In 1919, they
moved the business uptown and changed the name
slightly to The Norfolk Restaurant. It was in the
middle of the first block on the south side of Main
Street. Other enterprises were added. First was the Kandy
Kitchen, which was later sold to Mike Pete (Panayotis).
Then there was a bowling alley, poolroom and a barber
shop. Finally, there was the Imperial Theatre which
Angelo owned jointly with George Rollo. His brother,
Nick, went back to Greece in 1924.

When the Restoration began to move in 1928,
Angelo and his partners sold their property to that
organization.

Angelo Costas

Courtesy of Mr. Angelo Costas

A word of explanation concerning Merchant's
Square should be helpful at this point. There were
insufficient records to show what was in this block
during the colonial period so the restoration built
colonial style buildings on it and rented or leased
them to the merchants. Most of the buildings are
large and several of them joined together. Most of
them were completed in 1932.

It was in this year that Angelo opened the
Capitol Restaurant. He leased the newly constructed
quarters from the Restoration. Legions of William
and Mary students called the restaurant "The Middle
Greeks" since it was near the middle of the block.

Angelo and Tom Baltas married sisters from Richmond and they remained in business together until 1960.

It was in 1932 that Angelo, his cousin, George Stath, and George Rollo opened the new Imperial Theatre on the northwest corner of Boundary and Prince George Streets.

It was at this theatre that I saw my first movies. It was the era of the cowboys with white hats and white horses. Buck Jones, Tom Mix, Tim McCoy and Ken Maynard were the leading stars. Later Tarzan, King Kong and Frankenstein replaced the cowboys to some extent.

This theatre did not remain in operation, but two years since the Restoration opened the Williamsburg Theatre in its present location. At that time the town could not support two theatres. Angelo and his partners sold the building to the Restoration and it was converted into a two story structure with shops on the ground floor and rooms for rent on the second floor.

The Capitol Restaurant remained in operation by Angelo and his family until 1960, when he and Dora built the Colonial Motel on Richmond Road. They sold The Capitol, but it only remained in business with its new owners for a few years. Dora died in May of 1980, and Angelo still operates the motel at the age of 83 at this writing.

On the southeast corner of Main and Boundary Streets was "The Corner Greeks." It changed ownership several times through the years and the name changed with the ownership; but to the college students and many of the townspeople, it remained "The Corner Greeks."

One of the tenants here was Steve Sacalis. He operated the Williamsburg Restaurant on College Corner in the '40s. His first endeavor was The Palace Restaurant, opened after he came to town in 1930. It was near the Capitol Restaurant. After a few years, he established the Colonial Restaurant across the street which he operated until the '40s.

He and his wife, Chrysa, had owned and operated three flower shops in New York before coming

to Williamsburg. Although he was born in Greece,
Steve says he is only part Greek. The other parts
consist of Turkish and French. One of his ancestors
was married to a cousin of Lafayette, who was strand-
ed on a Greek island after his ship sank. In 1952,
Steve bought property from Rose Douglas on Richmond
Road and opened The Lafayette Restaurant which he
and "Mama" still operate today with the help of
their daughter, Betsy.

My family dealt with most of the merchants in
Williamsburg at one time or another during the '30s.
Among them were the Douglas' Bakery, later called
"The Pastry Shop", Hitchen's Store and Frazier-
Callis, now called  Frazier-Graves.

The Pastry Shop was close to me since a classmate of mine was the son of one of the owners. This
was Irvin Douglas, whose grandfather, W.A. Douglas,
established the business as Douglas' Bakery back in the
the early 1900's  Mr. Douglas' wife worked in the bakery
and they were known for their loud disagreements and
colorful behavior. Their son, Albert, who was Irvin's
father, also worked there and Irvin usually went to
the bakery from school each day. Irvin and I were
good friends, and I accompanied him to the bakery
quite often. Sometimes he would snitch doughnuts,
eclairs or other goodies for us and it was one of my
favorite stopping places after school.

When the elder Douglases grew too old to run the
bakery, Albert took over as manager. His wife, Rose,
also worked there as well as other relatives from time
to time. Irvin lived on Tyler Street, a short street
off of South England Street and sometimes I went home
with him after school.

One time my brother Clarence and I went home with
Irvin and we explored the garage. We found several
bottles of homemade wine and began to drink it. One
drink led to another until we were drunk. It was
winter and snow covered the ground. We left a rambling
trail of footprints in the snow as we staggered home.

We tried to hide our condition from Mom, but as
with most of our escapades we were far from successful.
Mom, however, was not as angry as we had supposed.
She tried to be firm with us but could not completely

conceal her amusement at our unusual condition. Irvin's
mother reacted in a similar manner, he told us next
day at school, but no more wine was left in the garage.

Mr. Webster Hitchens operated a grocery store on
the south side of Main street until the early '30 s.
It was located in the vicinity of the present reconstructed Music Shop. In 1933, he built a new building
on the northeast corner of Boundary and Prince George
Streets, across from the Imperial Theatre. The grocery
store was on the ground floor and was called West End
Market. The second floor was devoted to apartments.

Two of Mr. Hitchens' employees were Jim and John
Taylor, brothers who died many years ago. They lived
long enough to operate the West End Market. After John
died it was taken over by his son, John, Jr., or Buddy
as he was known.

Two doors west of the Capitol Restaurant was Bob
Wallace's College Shop. He was in an older building
before 1932, when the block was rebuilt. Behind the
College Shop was his Pocahontas Tea Room. He sold to
the Restoration officials and leased the same corner
from that organization. He operated a soda fountain and
bookstore on the corner for a few years, but later gave
this up to a series of Greeks for a restaurant. He
remained in the eastern half of the building with his
College Shop where he first concentrated on the college
trade by selling school supplies, pennants and souvenirs
of the college. As tourists began to come in increasing
numbers through the years, he added more items for that
trade. He also subleased a small part of his space in
the rear of the building for a bus station.

One of the stores on the north side of Main Street
was Frazier-Callis Co., a men's clothing store. It
had its beginnings on Downtown Main Street. A man
named Garner from Newport News ran it. When he closed
and returned to Newport News, one of his employees,
Allen Callis joined with Frazier to form Frazier-Callis.
They moved into Merchant's Square near the College.
In 1934, a young man named Leonard Graves went to work
there with the understanding that he would buy into
the business. Leonard was a native of Williamsburg,
born on Francis Street. His father died in 1934, and
he had to leave William and Mary and look for a job.

He began and remained at Frazier-Callis. He is still there at this writing. Around 1955, he changed the name to Frazier-Graves.

The oldest business concern in Williamsburg is the Bucktrout Funeral Service. The present owner, Clarence Page, Jr., has records showing that the business was established before 1759, making it the oldest mortuary concern in the United States.

It had its beginnings as a cabinet shop opened by Anthony Hay in the 1740's. He sold the shop in 1767, to Benjamin Bucktrout. Both men made caskets and this led Bucktrout into the funeral business. He moved the business to Francis Street, his business increased and he added other services, including house repairs.

The original Hay's Cabinet Shop has been reconstructed on Nicholson Street by Colonial Williamsburg.

The business remained in the Bucktrout family until 1928, when Horatio Bucktrout sold it to his nephew-in-law, Douglas Whitacre. In 1965 Whitacre sold it to Clarence Page, Jr.

The Richard Bland Tavern (at the sign of the Bull's Head) was owned and operated by Mrs. Virginia Haughwout, with the aid of her sister, Mrs. Ruth Peebles. They took in overnight guests, served meals and maintained a gift shop. They were members of an old Williamsburg family, the Braithwaites, who were related to the Bucktrouts.

Mrs. Haughwout, one of the town's more colorful characters, was dead set against the Restoration acquiring any of her extensive property, but they were able to lease it from her heirs through the Bucktrout-Braithwaite Foundation, established by Mrs. Haughwout. Today the Richard Bland has been restored and is called Wetherburn's Tavern.

More will be written about this family and its connections in the chapter entitled "Williamsburg Families."

Williamsburg's first motel was not called a motel and it was not in Williamsburg. It was Topping's Tourist Camp located just east of the city limits on Route 60. Built by William E. Topping in the 1920's, it was the first tourist facility on the Peninsula.

Mr. Topping was an oil distributor and was disturbed
by the lack of overnight accommodations in the vicinity
for his business associates so he decided to provide
them.

His first rooms were built in two log cabins.
Then there were rooms built end-to-end in a long
building and finally individual cabins were built.  A
small store and gas station sat at the entrance to
the facility which was later called Topping's Tourist
Inn.  Topping built a large home adjacent to the
tourist facility and when the latter was filled to
capacity, guests were taken into the home.  It was
called Rosemont reflecting the many rose bushes planted
along the highway between the tourist camp and the city
limits.

Originally from Poquoson, Topping built a summer
cottage in Dandy and he invited his family physician,
Dr. John Henderson, to build a cottage for himself on
Topping property.  Perhaps he considered having medical
attention readily available for his family while they
were in Dandy.

One of Mr. Topping's business ventures was a service
station and garage built on land belonging to C.T. Casey.
It was leased by R.W. Owens until the early '30s.
Topping subleased it from Owens but Owens operated it
for Topping.  It was on the southwest corner of Main
and Henry Streets.  Kenneth Chorley, the second president of the Restoration offered Topping the opportunity
to sell his lease.  He suggested that they flip a coin
for it, double or nothing, but Topping replied that
he could not gamble for such high stakes.  They tossed
for fun and Topping won.  He did sell his lease to
the Restoration later.

Mr. Topping was a dealer for the Shell Oil Co.
and on both sides of the entrance to the tourist camp
were shell-shaped lights atop pipes in a concrete and
pipe wall.  There were about a dozen of these lighted
globes each with the word SHELL across the top.  One
time a vandal with a slingshot or BB gun shot out the
S from each globe leaving a dozen HELL'S.  Of course,
they were quickly removed.

Chapter 7

TALES OF OLD WILLIAMSBURG

There had been stories told of the people and
events of Williamsburg for as long as I can remember.
In the process of collecting information for this
narrative I have heard others that are new to me.
The town has had several people with good memories
who liked to tell these stories. I knew most of them.

One of these story-tellers was Willard Gilley
who came to Williamsburg from Wisconsin in 1905. At
various times he explained the way things were
throughout his life until his death in September 1979.
He told about how important the railroad station was
in his early days since cars and trucks were few and
far between. Passenger travel as well as freight de-
pended almost entirely on the railroad, so the
station was a busy place.

Railroad Station before 1933

He told about its location at the end of North
England Street. It was a wooden building at first
which contained freight storage. A photo taken in
the late '20s shows it to be a brick building by that
time. When the Palace was built in the early '30s
the station was rebuilt in its present location at
the North end of Boundary Street and the old station
was removed along with the old knitting mill building and the Williamsburg Steam Laundry to make room
for the Palace gardens.

One story told by Gilley concerning the railroad
station involved a feud between the station agent,
Miles Shipman and A.W. Hitchens, owner of a grocery
and meat market on the lower end of Main Street.
It seems Mr. Hitchens was very concerned about meat
coming into the station from Richmond and Mr. Shipman
was not highly cooperative in keeping account of what
arrived or departed. This situation caused friction
between the two men.

Once when Hitchens called to ask if there was
meat at the station for him, Shipman told him, "No,
there's no meat here for you." Hitchens didn't believe this so he sent Jim Taylor in a truck to check
on it and he returned with the meat. This angered
Hitchens enough to call up and ask why he had been
told that there was no meat. Shipman replied, Well,
I didn't look and I don't care anyway!" Hitchens
then said, "Well Shipman, I don't give a damn about
you!" He then slammed the phone down and shortly
got a call from Shipman, who said, "I don't give a
damn about you either!"

Another story about Shipman and the telephone
was told in which Shipman changed his tune. His
custom was to answer the phone by shouting into it,

"Well?" Once it was answered by a co-worker, Mr. Cooper, who handed it to Shipman saying only, "It's for you." After yelling, "Well?" he discovered that it was Mrs. Shipman and she didn't like the way he answered the phone. He was heard to say in the next few minutes only "Yes, Ma'am" and "No Ma'am."

Another Gilley story taking place at the railroad station concerned a man named William Littlefield. He was the father of Mrs. E.M. Slauson of the colonial plantation known as "Powhatan Farm." Mr. Gilley described Littlefield as "a dour old fellow, not very accommodating to say the very best."

One time he drove his horse and buggy to the station to pick up some freight and tied the horse to a freight car on a siding. When he came out of the station, neither the freight car, the horse, nor the buggy were to be seen. The engine had hooked up to the freight car and hauled it off, dragging the horse and buggy almost into the coal dump. Mr. Littlefield of course was greatly upset but he got very little help or sympathy from those who saw the action.

Mr. Gilley told about another form of transportation, the old sailing vessels on the James River. He mentioned the sloops, schooners, scows, lighters and other types of working vessels plying local waters in earlier days. He described two of the local "sailing masters" or captains: Job L. Inman and W.T. Kinnamon. They were able and well respected citizens. Most long time residents of the town remember Captain Kinnamon as the owner of a garage on the northern side of Main Street near the Capitol. He sold to the Restoration and moved the business to Richmond Road where his son, Wilton, still operates it today.

The problems of sailing and local cargos of lumber and produce were covered by Mr. Gilley after which he related a story involving two brothers, Henry and David Cowles and "another old character by the name of Len Martin." These three men decided to sail a sloop full of watermelons from the Chickahominy River to Newport News, setting sail "about supper time."

After eating they apparently brought out the booze and all three slept it off without bothering to stand

watch. When they awoke next morning they were under
full sail but were in the same spot as the night before.
They had forgotten to lift the anchor and had sailed
around it all night.

Another teller of Williamsburg tales was Merlin
Larson. He grew up after the turn of the century and
remembered many things about life in pre-restoration
Williamsburg.

One of his stories concerns a well in the street
near the old Court House. It had been there since
the Civil War but was filled in just before World War
I. During the Battle of Williamsburg a Yankee officer
was watering his horse at the well when a shell exploded.
The sound scared the horse, causing it to jump and
throw the rider into the well. After that, the
townspeople would no longer drink from the well.

Mr. Dewey Renick could have qualified as a
teller of Williamsburg tales. He was born in Franklin
County, Virginia, and came to Williamsburg in 1915 to
attend William and Mary. He found employment at the
Williamsburg Female Institute, a girl's school owned
by the Norfolk Presbytery which stood where Matthew
Whaley now stands. His sister attended this school
while he worked there. His work included feeding the
pigs, milking the cows and helping on the farm which
was apparently behind the school.

It closed after he was there for a year so he
then found employment at Jack Spencer's Colonial Inn,
where Chowning's Tavern is now located. His brother
also worked there. It was a large three storied
structure built in 1895. In the times described by
Mr. Renick before World War I rooms were $1.50 and
meals 75 cents.

Renick told a story about two permanent residents
at the Inn, a Mrs. Scott and her daughter. One night
he was talking to Miss Scott in the lobby and she
expressed fear of finding a man in her room. She
then asked him to check the stove in her room. After
complying with her request "I conceived the idea of
running to my room and getting a pair of old pants in
which I stuffed some shirts in the legs, put shoes on
them and stuck them under her bed with the feet stick-
ing out." He had told Mrs. Scott about the action

52

and she thought it was a great joke. When Miss Scott went up to her room and saw the feet protruding from under the bed she came down screaming. Renick caught her at the foot of the stairs and she fainted in his arms. He ended by saying, "Had I not told her mother about it, I would have been in pretty much of a jam, perhaps but everything worked out all right."

Several stories were put into print by John S. Charles, a well-known and respected teacher and principal during the '20s.

One such story, written in a description of Main Street in the early years of the century, concerned a storekeeper named Jack Hudgins. His store was said to have been on the southwest corner of Nassau and Main Streets. Hudgins was known as "Old Jack" and. was described as "high tempered, irritable and very crabbed." A customer once came into the store and asked for meal (corn meal). While Hudgins was measuring it out, the customer mentioned that he was very glad to find meal since he had been all over town without finding any. Upon hearing this, Old Jack dropped the scoop back into the barrel and said, "If you went all over town before coming to my store you won't get any of this." As the angry customer left, Old Jack was "cussing a blue streak."

Jack Spencer's Colonial Hotel (Inn)

Another story related by Mr. Charles referred
to the "Peachy Block" (the present site of the James
Geddy House and Shop and the Norton-Cole House). On
this site once sat the store of Mr. P.T. Powell. His
cellar doors opened on the street, apparently the
only access to the cellar where "wet and dry groceries"
were kept. Whenever a clerk was down there he was at
the mercy of any "mischievous lad" who came along and
wanted to lock the cellar doors for fun. When this
was done it was to the dismay of the clerk below and
the waiting customer above. It is most probable that
this situation was not tolerated for very long.

The Peachy Block

One night in the late '20s a group of high school
boys raided a local watermelon patch. The group included a member of an old Williamsburg family, Aubrey
Skillman, our present-day Commissioner of Revenue.
After eating their full they lugged several left over
melons up on a railroad bridge just off Richmond Road
and dropped them on the tracks below. Sometime later
a train came along and the engineer seeing the gory
mess on the tracks jumped to an erroneous conclusion.
He pulled into the station and reported that he had
run over a bloody body. An investigation soon dis-
closed the "body" to be only the broken melons. The

culprits remained discreetly silent until the mess was forgotten.

Another story of the same period was told by Pete Hunt (Buster to his family). He remembers a boy by the name of Hensley Shea who was cavorting during a public affair one night at the old Williamsburg High School. There was an open vent to a heating duct with boxes piled under it making a convenient stairway to the open vent. It seems that the cover had been removed. Hensley ran up the box "steps" and jumped into the open vent. There was nothing to stop him and he slid down inside the duct and almost landed in the furnace, becoming stuck in a curve of the duct before reaching the furnace. The duct had to be dis-assembled to release Hensley. The affair took place in warm weather and the furnace was not fired up so the only harm done to Hensley was a few skinned places and a bad scare.

Williamsburg High School — 1921-1933

Several stories have circulated about John D.
Rockefeller, Jr. He would often stroll about town
during and after its restoration, observing the
activities of the residents.

Once he stopped in Bruton Parish Church to watch
a sign painter at work, putting names on the pews.
The painter was highly talented and well-known for
his signature left on signs all over town saying,
"Slater did it." After watching for a while,
Rockefeller asked Slater, "How many pews can you paint
in a day?"

Slater replied, "I don't know but it would be
more if I didn't have to stop and answer a lot of
damn fool questions!"

Rockefeller got the same type of reply from
Curly Atkinson, long time manager of Pender's and
Colonial Store. He came to town in 1936 from Suffolk
on a temporary assignment to manage one of Pender's
stores. Soon after his arrival he was supervising
the loading of stock into the basement window at
the rear of the store on Main Street. This was
accomplished by using a metal ramp to slide the stock
through a window. A stranger to Curly stopped to

Penders — "Curley's Store"

watch the efforts and finally asked, "Isn't there a
better way to do that job?" Curly didn't know he
was talking to John D. Rockefeller, Jr. when he replied, "Sure, but it's hard to get that damned
Restoration to do anything." Early next morning
workmen from the great corporation arrived to alter
the building any way that Curly wanted.

Curly, a very energetic and dedicated manager,
was proud of "his" store. It became the most adver-
tized Pender's store in the world due to an accidental
association with General Motors Corporation. The
auto firm decided to use the main business block of
Williamsburg as a backgroud for its photos of Buick
cars. They were parked in front of Curly's store
with the name "PENDER'S" clearly seen in the background. The promotion was worldwide and the store
benefited from the exposure.

It seems that "John D." got favored treatment
at least once in town. He was exceeding the speed
limits in the city and was stopped by W.H. Kelly,
our long-time police chief. For once, Kelly was at
a loss for words when he recognized the man he had
stopped. Rockefeller was apologetic and explained
that he was not used to driving in a place as small
as Williamsburg. Kelly let him go without even a
warning.

There are probably as many stories told about
Dr. Goodwin as there are about Rockefeller. One
such was about Dr. Goodwin preaching at Eastern State
Hospital. The ministers from the various churches
in town would take turns conducting the worship services at Eastern State in Cameron Hall. During one
of Dr. Goodwin's sermons after he had made a point,
a patient jumped up and exclaimed, "That's a lie!"

Another story about Dr. Goodwin was told shortly
after he returned to Williamsburg in 1923 as director
of the endowment fund and to teach religious education
at William and Mary. He was speaking to the faculty
which was presided over by Dr. J.A.C. Chandler. Dr.
Lesslie Hall, father of the later Mayor Channing M.
Hall, Sr., was in attendance. He was having trouble
with his furnace at home and arose to be excused. Dr.
Chandler thereby said, "Sit down, Dr. Hall, Dr.

Goodwin is not finished." After a while, as Goodwin went on and on, Dr. Hall arose again with the same admonition from Dr. Chandler. Finally, Hall arose and announced in a voice showing his irritation, "If I had Dr. Goodwin at home, I wouldn't need a furnace!"

"John D." was fond of remaining as inconspicuous as possible and he never wanted to announce his arrival in Williamsburg. One time, Rutherfoord Goodwin was interviewed by reporters who wanted to find out when Rockefeller was coming to town. They tricked him into telling them and a fuss was made when Rockefeller arrived. Consequently, "Ruddy" was reprimmanded for giving out confidential information.

Some Episcapalians want to be baptized by immersion as Baptists do instead of by sprinkling as is their usual way. When the rector received this kind of request from one of his parishioners, he usually contacted the minister of a local Baptist church to use its baptistry. One time while Dr. Goodwin was rector of St. Paul's Church in Rochester (1908-1923) a parishioner made such a request. Goodwin sought out a Baptist minister to use his church's facilities. The Baptist told him, "I'll furnish the tub but you'll have to do your own washing."

There was a time when Kenneth Chorley was President of the Restoration that he walked into a barbershop to get a haircut and found one of the Corporation's employees getting a haircut on company time. He objected to this and was asked by the employee, "Well, my hair grew on company time, didn't it?"

Another haircut story is told about a long-time Williamsburg barber, Bennie Newman. A customer got into his chair and announced to Bennie that he wanted a haircut but didn't want the usual conversation with it. Bennie reacted to this by replying, "Come with me." He led the man outside the shop and pointed up the street, saying, "See that shop? They give haircuts without conversation. I don't!"

The final tale of this chapter is set in a later period than the rest of this narrative but I feel that it is too interesting to omit. I sincerely hope that the reader will agree.

Tom Miller was a guide at Bruton Parish Church and he requested that he be buried there. He was cremated and the Reverend Francis Craighill decided to honor his request. However, he did not ascertain the wishes of the vestry. He apparently thought they might object since under cover of darkness he sought the aid of the verger, a colored man by the name of Lem Jones, and entered Bruton's graveyard. Equipped only with a flashlight and a post-hole digger they went to work. A small hole was dug and Mr. Miller's ashes were lowered into the undersized grave.

Somehow a relative in Maryland discovered the burial, and wrote to the vestry asking that a marker be placed upon Miller's grave. A church official, not knowing about the midnight burial, wrote back that there must be some mistake. Someone in the vestry said, "Let's ask Lem." "Yes," he replied to the question, "He's buried over by the wall."

Virginia law forbids the moving of a grave except by court order. The vestry, therefore, decided that they had little choice but to provide a marker for Mr. Miller's grave. He died in 1956.

Chapter 8


WILLIAMSBURG FAMILIES (OLD & NOT SO OLD)


As in any town, large or small, Williamsburg has
had people and families come and go. Some only stay for
a few years while others stay for hundreds of years. The
oldest family I know about is the Peachy family. The
earliest date on the tombs of Cedar Grove Cemetary is on
that of COL Thomas Griffin Peachy (1734-1810). He seems
to be the first of the Peachys to come to Williamsburg,
probably from Richmond County, where the name is spelled
in the records Peachey. He died in Williamsburg. The
first immigrant, Samuel Peachy settled in Richmond County
along the banks of the Rappahannock River in 1659. Thomas
G. Peachy was the great grandson of Samuel the immigrant.
The records can be easily confused since there are several
people of each of these names as in so many families. Most
of our ancestors showed little imagination in naming their
children. This adds difficulty to the work of the genea-
logist.
Most of the Williamsburg Peachys attended William
and Mary. Thomas G. Peachy II was listed as a student
there in 1812. William S. Peachy was so listed between
1785 and 1790. B. D. Peachy I was listed twice--once
from 1866 to 1868 and again from 1870 to 1877. B. D.
Peachy, Jr. was listed in 1914. B. D. Peachy III broke
with tradition and attended V.P.I. He has a son who is
B. D. Peachy IV.
The third son of Thomas G. Peachy, William S.
Peachy, married Mary Monro Cary, who lived in the
Peachy-Randolph House and offered it to General
Lafayette when he visited Williamsburg in 1824. The
house is now called the Peyton Randolph House.
My contacts with this family were twofold. As

mentioned at the beginning of this book my family lived
in a house owned by the Peachy family. There were two
houses separated by two shops, all attached and called,
"The Peachy Block." The house facing Courthouse Green
was the home of B. D. Peachy Sr. who died in 1916. His
wife, the former Mary Garnett Lane, died in 1929. Their
home is today called the Norton-Cole House.

One of my classmates and friends was Bathurst
Daingerfield Peachy III, who like his father was called
Bat by friends. B. D. Peachy, Jr. was Williamsburg's
Commonwealth Attorney in the '30s. B. D. Peachy Sr. was also
an attorney. In 1900 he was named to the committee to
urge the celebration of the founding of Jamestown, which
was accomplished in 1907. His fellow townsmen on the
committee were Lyon G. Tyler, Reverend W. T. Roberts,
Professor T. J. Stubbs, Henry D. Cole, J. B. C. Spencer
and John S. Charles. All were among Williamsburg's most
distinguished citizens of that day.

With the departure of Mrs. B. D. Peachy Jr. to be
near a son in Suffolk recently, there is now no longer
a Peachy living in Williamsburg.

Peachy

Courtesy of Daily Press
"Miss Ginny"

Mention has been made previously of the Braithwaite
and Bucktrout families. Both have been in the Williamsburg
area since colonial times. Both were in the funeral
business. Mrs. Virginia Braithwaite Haughwout (pronounced
Howard) whom I knew and served as an artist, was a
Braithwaite. Her mother, Mrs. W. H. Braithwaite, was a
Bucktrout and operated a funeral business established in
1823. She also managed a business called Braithwaite's

Broker's Supply Company which was on Main Street in 1898. At one time she sold brass door knockers in the old Powder Horn.

I was aware of Mrs. Haughwout and her "Bull's Head Tavern" long before I became acquainted with her. She acquired the building from Miss Kitty Morecock in 1921 and "Miss Kitty" operated a Tea Room in the Tavern for a few years after selling it. This was a place for serving tea and light refreshments. (The term Tea Room seems to be fading from use today.) In the late '40s when I first worked for Mrs. Haughwout, called "Miss Ginny" by many of the townspeople, she was operating the Richard Bland Tavern with the aid of her sister, Mrs. Ruth Peebles and a few part time colored helpers. She discovered that I was an artist and a sign painter, and she summoned me to the "Bull's Head" as many people called her place. If Mr. Nelson was the most memorable male character I remember, certainly "Miss Ginny" was his female counterpart.

She dressed as many ladies of her age did in those days, perhaps a little old fashioned, even then. She usually wore an apron. She called me to do art work for her but she expressed interest in me as a person. She wanted to know about my family, my college studies, how long I had been in Williamsburg. In return she told me something about herself and her antique building. She left no doubt that she was greatly interested in her town and her state.

She usually sat herself in the gift shop room, near the fireplace, and I remember with pleasure the fragrance of the woodsmoke mingled with the smell of country ham from the tea room. Things were not always in perfect order in her shop. It had that "lived in" look but it was cozy and she seemed to know where everything was located. She was very much in command of the place as I could see when her sister or the employees came to her with a problem or questions. She answered them and issued orders in a most firm and positive manner. Her business ability was somewhat evident when a price was set for my work. She liked to bargain and after I became aware of this I would start high and allow her to talk me down to what I needed to profit from my work. This seemed to be a mutually satisfactory arrangement.

One of the tasks I performed for Mrs. Haughwout was to repaint the bull's head on the sign in front of her place. Every few years it would need touching up. She also had me paint a coat of arms on a wooden plaque or shield for each of her ancestors and perhaps some who were not related to her. Included were the names of Ballard, Bland, Bruce, Braithwaite, Nelson, Haughwout and Higgins. She fussed at me a little bit because the Higgins' arms had three black crow's heads on a green background and was not as handsome as some of the others.

Haughwout

In the late '40s she bought a colonial plantation house in Providence Forge and had it moved to Williamsburg. It was placed and refurnished on a section of her land on the south side of Francis Street adjacent to the Williamsburg Inn. It was called Providence Hall.

Officials of Colonial Williamsburg made attempts to buy her property, especially the Richard Bland Tavern but she was determined not to let them have it. She specified in her will that none of her property was to be sold.

She died in 1957 and her heirs held on to the property for a few years but they finally leased it to Colonial Williamsburg for 99 years. The Richard Bland became Wetherburn's Tavern after being carefully restored by Colonial Williamsburg. It is well-kept and well-furnished but lacks the charm it had when it smelled of wood smoke and country ham.

Mrs. Haughwout established the Bucktrout-Braithwaite Foundation through which she sought to preserve her holdings and have them used as she saw fit. Following is a section of the by-laws, officers, et cetera of the Foundation.

BY-LAWS OF THE BUCKTROUT-BRAITHWAITE MEMORIAL FOUNDATION

---

Article 1   Objects and purposes of Corporation

To receive donations by gift, or will of real or personal property and to own, operate, use, and develop the same, and to devote the proceeds and avails thereof for any and all of the following:

(1)   To promote a greater interest in Protestant religious education among the youth of America,

(2)   To establish at Williamsburg, Virginia, the Bucktrout-Braithwaite Episcopal School for the education of children under the auspices of the Protestant Episcopal Church,

(3)   To preserve, after the death of Virginia Braithwaite Haughwout, as a self supporting and independent unit all the historic sites and buildings owned by Virginia Braithwaite Haughwout in the city of Williamsburg, Virginia, during her lifetime and in the care of the property to carry out the principles of the Association for the Preservation of Virginia Antiquities.

(4)   To maintain, improve, and develop as an American shrine and as a memorial to Virginia Braithwaite Haughwout the building at Williamsburg, Virginia, known as Providence Hall.

(5)   To establish a museum to contain old family heirlooms of the Bucktrout and Braithwaite families, and other loans, purchases, and gifts of early Americana, and

(6)   To promote, by the teaching of youth, the democratic principles proclaimed in the Constitution

of the United States, the ethical and religious teachings of the Protestant Episcopal Church, and good manners, chivalry, courtesy, and gentility.

In furtherance of the foregoing objects, the said corporation may:

Subscribe to, purchase or otherwise acquire, hold and deal in, sell, assign, transfer, mortgage, pledge or otherwise dispose of shares of the capital stock, and of the bonds, securities or other evidences of debt created and issued by any other corporation, company, or association.

May borrow money upon resolutions of its Board of Trustees in accordance with the statutes of Virginia necessary for the purposes of the corporations NOTES, obligations or bonds thereof and secure the payment of same by mortgage or deed of trust on its property, real or personal, or any part thereof.

The affairs of the corporation shall be managed by a Board of not less than five or more than twenty Trustees. Vacancies in the Board of Trustees caused by expiration of term of office, death, resignation, or removal shall be filled by the Board of Trustees, with preference given, if practicable, to the children of Virginia Braithwaite Haughwout, to her grandchildren, and to decendants of the Bucktrouts and Braithwaites of Williamsburg in this order.

The names and residences of the Trustees who are to manage the affairs for the first year of its existence, and until their successors are elected and qualified, together with the names and residences of the officers of the corporation, are as follows:

OFFICERS:

President: Virginia B. Haughwout . . Williamsburg
Virginia

Vice President: R. Nelson Smith. . . Yorktown
Virginia

Treasurer: Anne Ballard Cutler . . . Williamsburg
Virginia

Secretary: Anne Ballard Cutler . . . Williamsburg
Virginia

TRUSTEES:

Virginia B. Haughwout . . . . . . . . Williamsburg
Virginia

Anne Ballard Cutler . . . . . . . . . Williamsburg
Virginia

Virginia Bruce Rodarmor . . . . . . . New York City
New York

Lefferd Braithwaite Haughwout . . . . Elyria
Ohio

Alexander B. Haughwout. . . . . . . . Bryan River
Connecticut

R. Nelson Smith . . . . . . . . . . . Yorktown
Virginia

Horatio M. Peebles. . . . . . . . . . Norfolk
Virginia

Churchill B. Rugg . . . . . . . . . . Arlington
Virginia

William Henry Braithwaite . . . . . . Northridge
California

Frances L. Saks . . . . . . . . . . . Oak Ridge
Tennessee

Mrs. Ronald Ross. . . . . . . . . . . San Diego
California

The corporation may from time to time create such
additional officers as may be necessary or convenient for
the conduct of its business and may organize such commit-
tees as it may determine necessary, with such authority
and duties as may be legally delegated.

Most of the officers listed above are deceased.
The Foundation was incorporated in 1954. It seems to
be somewhat dormant in recent years.

A portion of Mrs. Haughwout's land behind Providence Hall is not covered in the lease the same way the remainder of it is. This includes her grave. The tombstone reads:

SIT AND REST A WHILE

VIRGINIA BRAITHWAITE HAUGHWOUT

February 17, 1876

June 24, 1957

I loved Virginia

Next to her grave is a flat stone erected by Mrs. Haughwout in 1953 which reads, "To honor the soldiers of the American Revolution buried here--names unknown."

Near this spot is a pauper's graveyard where a deal was made in the early '30s between the city and Bucktrout Funeral Home to bury people with no funds or relatives.

After Mrs. Haughwout died in 1957 her sister, Mrs. Peebles, moved from the "Bull's Head" and had me undertake various decorative tasks for her. She was as friendly as her sister but not as dominant a personality. We often talked about her family. I attended school with her youngest son, Horatio, whose nickname was "Snitz." He was a couple of years older than me and was a junior at William and Mary in 1942. I don't remember whether or not the draft got him before graduation. His father, Peter Paul Peebles was a professor of law at William and Mary.

Some of the names of other families who lived in Williamsburg for several generations or more were Armistead, Binns, Bowry, Bozarth, Brooks, Caldwell, Casey, Christian, Clark, Clowes, Cole, Douglas, Foster, Garrett, Geddy, Gilliam, Gore, Griffin, Hall, Henderson, Holmes, Johnston, Larson, Mahone, Maupin, Maynard, Mepham, Morris, Nightengale, Opheim (pronounced Opine), Rogers, Saunders, Slauson, Spencer, Vaiden and Warburton.

Names of some members of old families with whom
I attended school who lived for the most part in James
City County were Cowles, Minor, Richardson, and Waltrip.

There was a man named Leakey who managed a roof
repair business in the'30s. The shop was on Webster
Street. I believe this was once in Ripley's "Believe It
or Not" newspaper feature.

There was a family living in town in the'30s of
whom I knew only one member. The family was Blacknall
and the one I knew was Johnny. His father was John T.
Blacknall who was the manager of VEPCO or Williamsburg
Power Company as it was first called. Mr. Blacknall was
a member of the Pulaski Club until his death in 1928. He
left Johnny and his sister Margaret as orphans. Johnny
was a likable lad and was taken in by Mr. and Mrs.
Spafford Timberlake. He was the Commissioner of
Revenue for the town. They sent Johnny to Christ Church,
a private school. Later he worked at the uptown Rexall
and was well-known to most town residents. World War II
came along and Johnny went to war. He never came back

The Firehouse
England Street
The Early '20s

VEPCO office
The Late '20s

but the local V.F.W. Post was named for him and another
local lad who never returned, Phil Chess.

A family which has been in Williamsburg for over
a hundred years is the Bowry family. I went to school
with James B. Bowry, who is the last one bearing the
name still residing in the Williamsburg area. His
brother and sisters live in the Newport News area. Their
father and grandfather both worked at Eastern State
Hospital. They lived on Ireland Street. Their great
grandfather came from Charles City County. Their father
was James Leonard Bowry. Their grandfather was Bushrod
Washington Bowry who in 1884 bought a lot in the
vicinity of Chowning's Tavern. It was the same lot that
was later sold to Jack Spencer for his Colonial Inn.
B. D. Peachy Sr. was Bowry's attorney in the transaction.
Bushrod's nephew was James Walter Bowry called "Red
Headed" Jim. He was the Sergeant-at-Arms of the Pulaski
Club in 1920.

The Clowes family lived on Ireland Street in
a house said to have been constructed of bricks brought
from England at the same time as those brought over for
the building of Bruton Parish Church. One of my schoolmates was John A. Clowes. We called him Johnny. He was
larger than most of us and was a good athlete. He
played football for William and Mary and was on the
1942 squad. His two sisters who still live in the area
at this writing are Mrs. Mattie Vaughn and Mrs. Gertrude
Holland. Their father was John H. Clowes and their
grandfather was Alexander Texas Clowes. The latter's
brother Peter once owned most of the land and houses
on Ireland Street. After living here he moved to
Norfolk.

Related to the Clowes family was the Badkins
family as could be suspected by the name of a younger
schoolmate and friend of mine by the name of Texas
Slaughter Badkins.

Another family I have known most of my life is
the Clark family, especially three of the four children
of Frank R. Clark and Irene C. Hogg Clark. These were
Fannie Badkins Clark, Anna K. Clark (Nancy) and James W.
Clark (Jay). Fannie married Lort Nightengale. Nancy
married Paul Griesenaur Jr. and Jay married Janet Jolly.
I don't remember the oldest son, Franklin L. Clark.

The Clark family has been in Williamsburg for many generations. Fannie and her brothers and sister were born in the Walthall House which was on the corner of Boundary and Francis Streets. Their great grandmother Clark was Parkey Jane Walthall before marrying their great grandfather Thomas L. Clark(e).

Lort Nightengale's (called Lit by family and close friends) great grandfather was Kryn Nightengale who came from Holland and landed in New York in 1855. His grandfather, Cornelius was born there the same year. In 1869 they moved to Virginia and settled on a small part of a 1200-acre farm called "Piney Grove," in James City County. Here was where "Lit" was born. His father, Robert Cornelius, was born at "Blue Bottom" also in James City County.

Mention has been made of Mary Wall Christian, long-time art teacher at Mathew Whaley School and John S. Charles. The latter was Mary Wall's grandfather. Her father was Hodges Christian. When she taught me in her art classes she lived on the southwest corner of Nassau and Prince George Streets. The elevated area of her home was called "Buttermilk Hill" since this commodity was once sold there, according to her grandfather Charles. He was affectionately called "Professor Charles" but was a beloved teacher and principal for many years. He was active in the events of the town and was a member of the Pulaski Club.

Mary Wall's Aunt Emily Christian held several positions at William and Mary from 1902 to 1934. Among them were: Secretary, Assistant Librarian and Librarian.

One of the oldest families with a descendant still living in Williamsburg is the Tucker-Coleman family. Much has been written about this family. Most of them were leaders, teachers, lawyers, ministers, soldiers and writers.

The first to arrive in Virginia was St. George Tucker who came from Bermuda in 1770. In 1788 he bought the property where the present St. George Tucker House sits. He moved an older building from Palace Green-- thought to be Levingston House--to his newly purchased lot and began to enlarge it. He was a lawyer, judge and professor of law at William and Mary.

His second son, Nathaniel Beverley Tucker, acquired the house at the death of his father in 1827.  Like his father he eventually taught law at William and Mary. Beverley's daughter, Cynthia, next inherited the house. She first married Henry Washington and after he died she married Charles W. Coleman.  Their third son, George P. Coleman, then inherited the house.  Like his forebears he attended William and Mary.  He organized the Virginia Department of Highways and was mayor of Williamsburg from 1929 to 1934.  His daughter, Janet Coleman Kimbrough, lives in the old house today.  She is a retired physician and keeper of the family history and tradition.

Chapter 9


WILLIAM AND MARY


Much has been written about the old college and
there is little original material that I can furnish but
I shall attempt to present a view of it as I saw it plus
a few of its instructors and by-gone incidents.

The college has been an important part of my
life since I roamed its campus as a youngster, was graduated
from it in 1948 and still use some of its facilities
today.  I knew several members of the faculty quite well
even before I began to study there in the fall of 1941.

The college has always been a prominent part of
Williamsburg and most long-time residents will tell us
that there has always been a warm and friendly feeling
between the townspeople and the students, in spite of
an occasional prank or misunderstanding.

Quite a few students through the years have
roomed in local homes as in most college towns and many
long-time friendships have resulted.

Very little can be written about William and
Mary during the '20s and '30s without mention of its dyna-
mic president, Julian Alvin Carrol Chandler.  He became
president in 1919 and guided the college in an inspired
manner until his death in 1934.  He was blunt, energetic,
and financially adept, and under his leadership the
college grew to proportions which were surprising
even to those who knew him well.  Under his guidance
4.5 million dollars were spent to build most of the
buildings, with which I was familiar as I grew up.
These included dormitories, classroom buildings, sorority
houses, and the infirmary.

Enrollment increased from 189 in 1919 to 3,758 by
1933 including the branch schools he established.  These

began in 1933 in Norfolk and Richmond as the Norfolk
Division of William and Mary and Richmond Professional
Institute.  They have grown tremendously and today have
become Old Dominion University (ODU) and Virginia
Commonwealth University (VCU).

The year 1926 is known as the year in which Dr.
Goodwin first spoke to Rockefeller about his dream of
restoring Williamsburg.  Dr. Chandler, who selected
Goodwin to head the endowment fund and to teach religious
education, participated in a ceremony that same year which
was long remembered by those who attended.

On the southwest corner of Boundary Street and
Jamestown Road was a flagpole with a brick support and
a bench all around its base.  It was there as far back
as my memory goes and like so many long-time fixtures,
little attention was paid to it.  Research reveals
that it was given to William and Mary in a presentation ceremony on September 26, 1926 by the Ku Klux
Klan.  It was accepted for the college by President
Chandler.

Articles in the press at the time pointed out
that Chandler had little choice in accepting the gift
which was given "decently and in good temper."  If
he had "spurned the gift and scorned the givers" it
might be difficult in the future to speak for the
principles for which the flag stands.  However, Dr.
Chandler showed little mercy in his acceptance
speech.

After hearing the words of the Imperial
Wizard of the KKK, Dr. Hiram Evans, in which he identi-
fied William and Mary with the birth of principles
found in the Constitution, Chandler began his speech.
He noted first that a recent Klan circular had stated
that the Klan agreed that the Declaration of
Independence was the basis of popular government.
"Would that every American would hold this view,
and in holding this view would not be content with
the mere expression of this view, but would put into
practice this ideal, not only as an individual but
in all his group connections, for sometimes men
declare one thing and practice another."

This was only the beginning of Chandler's
berating of the Klan.  After listing some of the

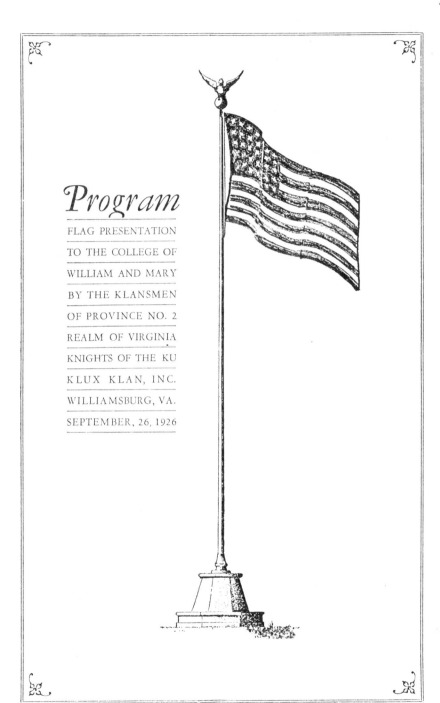

*Program*

FLAG PRESENTATION

TO THE COLLEGE OF

WILLIAM AND MARY

BY THE KLANSMEN

OF PROVINCE NO. 2

REALM OF VIRGINIA

KNIGHTS OF THE KU

KLUX KLAN, INC.

WILLIAMSBURG, VA.

SEPTEMBER, 26, 1926

landmarks of American freedom such as the Bill of
Rights, he lectured on their meaning and included
a portion which dealt with "Christian forebearance,
love and charity toward each other." He concluded
with a quote from one of the Klan's ideals: "We
stand for the enforcement of law by the regularly con-
stituted authorities. This order does not take the
law into its own hands, and will not tolerate acts
of lawlessness on the part of its members."

Dr. Chandler went on and on in this fashion.
It can be assumed that the Imperial Wizard and
his supporters were squirming in their seats,
regretting the day they decided to honor the old
college with its feisty president.

Embedded in the brick base of the flagpole was
a metal plaque commemorating the presentation of the
gift to the college by the Klan. Through the years
this plaque was the target of many college pranks.
At least once it was cemented over. It was finally
removed. The pole and its base were all removed
about 1955.

During Chandler's term in office he became enraged
with George Rollo when he moved the Imperial Theater
from Main Street to the corner of Boundary and Prince
George Streets in 1932. Chandler restricted the girls
to one block from the college after dark so they could
not attend movies at the new location. He had films
shown in the Phi Beta Kappa Hall to compensate the students but it was not a highly satisfactory arrangement.

Part of Chandler's efforts to build up William
and Mary included building the faculty. He added new
courses for them to teach along the way. I attended
school with the children of most of the professors
engaged by Chandler. Some of these included Donald
Davis, Joseph Geiger, Wayne Gibbs, Jess Jackson,
Richard Morton, Robert Robb, Pelzer Wagener, and Dudley
Woodbridge.

Dr. Woodbridge was one of the most widely known
and best loved professors at the college. Born in
Ohio and raised in Seattle, he arrived at William and
Mary in 1927 and became an assistant professor the
same year. He rose rapidly and by 1942 was acting

dean of the Department of Jurisprudence (the former name
of the Law School). He became dean of the Law School in
1953. He was a member of Phi Beta Kappa and the American
Bar Association among many other organizations. He was
the first recipient of the Thomas Jefferson Award in 1963.

Courtesy of Mrs. Julia Oxrieder
Dr. Woodbridge

Courtesy of William & Mary Alumni Gazette
Chandler, Popp and Kent

His professional accomplishments were quite
impressive but they were equaled by his efforts
as a humanitarian. He could always be counted on to
give extra help to anyone needing it in class or out.
His kindness to all was well known, especially to the
neighborhood children. His daughter, Julia, was a
classmate of mine and I was acquainted with the rest of
his family. I saw Dr. Woodbridge around town helping
his children with the newspapers they delivered. I
observed him in winter helping children who were
skating on Lake Matoaka. Many of these children, long
since grown, remember his kindness. He kept 16 pairs
of ice skates to lend to youngsters and although he
didn't skate himself he maintained a fire on the lake-
shore and kept a watchful eye on the young skaters.

In the early '60s Dr. Woodbridge built a fall-
out shelter for the neighborhood women and children. It
was built under the yard, was reached from the basement
of the house and the neighbors were invited to stock
it with food and medical supplies.

Another William and Mary professor I knew was
Donald Davis, under whom I took a biology class. He
was at the college continuously from 1916, except for
1917 and 1918 when he was a first lieutenant of infantry.
He was head of the Department of Biology for many years
and was responsible for starting freshman biology students

making insect collections.  They could be seen all over
town in the fall and spring capturing their specimens
each with a "butterfly net" in one hand and holding
their duc-caps on with the other.

Dr. Davis was the founder of the Virginia
Fisheries Lab which today has become the Virginia
Institute of Marine Science.

He once acquired some unexpected lab animals.
It seems that Charlie Duke, bursar at the college on a
trip to Florida, acquired two monkeys from an unknown
source and not knowing what to do with them upon his
return to Virginia, he presented them to Dr. Davis.
Why they were collected by Mr. Duke was never ascer-
tained,

Dr. Davis died in 1950 and in 1970 a bronze
tablet was created by sculptor, Carl Roseberg, honoring
Davis and installed in Millington Hall where the
Biology Department is now housed.

I never took classes under Dr. Daniel J.
Blocker, but I was well-acquainted with him through the
Williamsburg Baptist Church where he was once the pastor.
During my attendance at the church after it was built
in 1934 on Richmond Road, I believe Dr. Blocker was a
substitute pastor through the years.  His full time job
was as head of the Sociology Department at the college.

Born in Starke, Florida in 1874, he came to
William and Mary in 1921.  His fierce countenance masked
a kind and friendly personality.  He will be long remembered at William and Mary and at Williamsburg Baptist
Church.

One of the arts I needed in order to major in
Fine Art was Theater.  I was lucky enough to have a
little of its history taught to me by the founder and
long-time Director of the William and Mary Theater,
Althea Hunt.  A native of Conneaut, Ohio, she was
brought to the college in 1926 by Dr. Chandler and was
the director of the theater until 1957.  She directed
the Common Glory outdoor drama in its first year, 1947.

The theater which Miss Hunt directed so long
was housed in the old Phi Beta Kappa building until it
was left homeless by a fire in 1953.  Miss Hunt helped
in planning the construction of the new Phi Beta Kappa

Memorial Hall which opened in 1957. It must have given her great pleasure to be involved in this project since she was a member of the Phi Beta Kappa Society which was founded at William and Mary in 1776.

She was succeeded as director of the theater by one of her students, Howard Scammon. She retired from all duties in 1961 and died in 1971.

One of the college professors I knew best was Dr. James D. Carter. He was associated with William and Mary for over forty years. He and my father served in the same Army unit during World War I. He was the company barber for a while and Dad told me about some of his escapades. "J. D." as Dad called him seemed to have a knack for languages and picked up the French language at amazing speed. This enabled him to deal very well with the French girls and he became the envy of his buddies. His war-time experiences in France very likely caused him to take an interest in French and other languages that was to last a lifetime.

After the war in 1919, he entered William and Mary. After returning to France to receive a doctorate from the University of Toulouse, in 1927 he began his teaching career at William and Mary.

Dr. Carter's extensive travels put him in great demand as a speaker and he could be counted on as such, especially in Williamsburg. One of his favorite organizations was the American Legion, which he served for many years. For several of these years he was commander of the local Post 39 from which he received a citation for service in 1973.

His "second" language was Spanish and this led him to make several trips to Mexico. From these trips he was inspired to write a book "Going to a Bullfight? How to Understand and Enjoy Every Phase of It." He also wrote a book in Spanish--"Baseball Vocabulary."

Another long time member of the William and Mary faculty was Charles Marsh, professor of economics who came to the college in 1930 from Wisconsin. He stayed until 1958 when he accepted a position as president of Wofford College in Spartanburg, South Carolina. He returned to William and Mary in 1968 and retired in 1973.

An active member of the Methodist Church, he
preached the morning service once in 1937 in place of
the local minister, Reverend T. J. Hawkins.

He remembers another incident from the '30s
that was not as pleasant as the one above. He and
Mrs. Marsh were living on Prince George Street when
Dr. Smoot's cook came to the door for help. She had
been shot while waiting for a bus in the neighborhood.
Her jealous lover had mistakenly thought she had taken
up with another man. She recovered from her wounds
but the innocent man with her died from gunshot wounds
received in the incident.

Another member of Phi Beta Kappa Society among
William and Mary's faculty was Dr. Robert Robb. From
Caroline Co., he was graduated from William and Mary in
1893 and received his M.A. from the University of Virginia
in 1900. He began to teach at William and Mary in 1918
and became head of the Chemistry department in 1924. In
1940 he received the Alumni Medallion. He retired in 1946
and died in 1951.

Dr. Robb was a descendant of Pocahontas and John
Rolfe. He was married in 1927. He and Mrs. Robb were
living in the Ludwell-Paradise House in 1928 when they
were asked to move by Dr. Goodwin who had bought the old
building for Williamsburg Holding Corporation. It was the
first of many purchases by Goodwin for future restoration.
Dr. Robb then bought a home on Chandler Court from Mrs.
Ballard, a cousin of Dr. Goodwin. It was next door to the
home of Dr. John Garland Pollard, who taught Government at
William and Mary and who was later governor of Virginia.
He was Mayor of Williamsburg in 1928-29.

Another long-time member of the college faculty
was Glenwood Clark who joined the English department in
1920. He taught American Literature, Journalism and
Creative Writing. His students have said that he had a
special gift of communication and could make literature
come alive and cause young minds to think creatively.

Mr. Clark retired in 1954 and died in 1967. He
is survived by Mrs. Clark, still living in Williamsburg,
and one son, Gary who was a few years behind me in school.

Since I majored in Fine Arts at William and
Mary, it is only fitting that some mention be made of

one of the instructors therein. Most of my art classes
were taken under Thomas E. Thorne since he taught so many
of them. I remember particularly the classes in painting
and art history.

Thorne was a native of Maine and was well-
established as an artist before coming to the college in
1940. Three years later he became head of the department. He painted his first public works at the age
of 12 and by 1930 was first listed in Who's Who in American Art.

I became well-acquainted with him through taking
his classes and helping him with displays. The college
owned a large and valuable collection of Chinese Art
which was displayed in Barrett Hall. I was asked to
help him rotate this collection from time to time since
it was too large to display all at once. He also asked
my assistance in setting up displays of paintings
periodically in several areas of the campus. I remember
questioning him as to the value of some of them since a
few looked somewhat simple and amateurish to me. His
answers, to the best of my recollection, can be summed
up thusly--"Its all a matter of overall design and
color. Each artist sees things, at least slightly,
differently and must be allowed to express himself
accordingly."

I thoroughly enjoyed the classes taken under Tom
Thorne. He could make it fun; whether teaching a student how to apply colors on a canvas or lecturing on the
merits of Cezanne, Renoir or Picasso. His knowledge of
the personal lives of the artists enabled him to inject
into his lectures interesting tidbits as the sexual
adventures of some of them. This kept even the most
uninterested student wide awake.

Another long time member of the William and Mary
staff whom I knew quite well for many years was
Yelverton O. Kent. He first came to the college in 1918
as a member of the Student Army Training Corps which had
its headquarters at William and Mary. After service in
the Army and working in Norfolk, he returned to the college and received his B.S. in 1931. A very active student, he was president of his sophomore and junior
classes and received letters in five sports.

Before graduation he took flying lessons,

becoming one of four students selected to learn how to fly. He then became an instructor at the school. In 1933, he courted the former Elizabeth Cleveland by moonlight flying and made her Mrs. Y. O. Kent. She had a younger brother, Everett, who lived with the Kents for a few years while going to Matthew Whaley High School. I knew him then but it was when we both attended William and Mary that we became fast friends.

When Yel Kent taught flying, he lived in the President's House and Chandler gave him room, board, and laundry service. The next year he was paid 30 dollars a month. He became manager of the college airport. Later he managed the college dining hall. In a corner of this facility, he established a small bookstore which grew in size until the present separate building was built in 1966 on Jamestown Road. He was in charge of the bookstore until his retirement in 1971. While he was managing the dining hall, he had occasion to appoint a waiter for President Chandler. It was none other than Davis Y. Paschall, future President of William and Mary.

"Yel" Kent's sporting activities at William and Mary led to his induction into the William and Mary Athletic Hall of Fame in 1970. In 1971, he was honored as an emeritus member in the National Association of College Stores. In recognition of his services to William and Mary, he was awarded the Alumni Medallion at the homecoming ceremonies of 1977.

Kent took an active interest in his town. He served for 14 years as a member of City Council. He was president of the Rotary Club and Governor of the Loyal Order of Moose, soon after its charter in the early '50s. I was a charter member of this organization when Kent became Governor and I remember him as a good-humored, friendly fellow who could always be counted on to take a leading part in any activity.

The flight school in which Kent had an early connection was one of the innovations of President Chandler. It was the result of a bargain made between him and Raymond Riordan of New York who ran a school for young men on a ship docked at Jamestown. Riordan used the laboratories of William and Mary, and in return taught four students to fly. Chandler soon initiated the

aeronautics program at the college. He hired Col. Earl
Popp from the Riordan School to direct the program and
appointed his son, Julian Chandler, and Kent as two of
Popp's instructors. This became the first Department of
Aeronautics of any American college.

Their equipment included two open cockpit
biplanes, a 2-seat fleet trainer, and a high-wing, 3-place
Curtiss monoplane. They had a lab for overhauling
engines in the basement of Rogers Hall, and, later, a
hanger was built.

Students received no credit for flying, but the
college gave credit for the ground school curriculum
that included aeronautics, celestial navigation,
mechanics and the theory of flight.

Most of the student fliers belonged to a Flight
Club and rented the planes from the Department of
Aeronautics for club work.

Some of the pilots would fly to Jamestown and on
the way back would cut their engines and glide silently
over Barrett Hall where girls some times sunbathed nude
on the roof. It was called "Barrett Beach."

Highlights of the flight school activities
included visits by Senator Hiram Bingham, the chairman
of a Senate Committee on Aeronautics, and Amelia Earhart.
Col. Popp presented Miss Earhart with a flight Club pin.
Another highlight was the winning of the Loening Trophy,
recognizing William and Mary's as the best flight program
in the country.

Another woman involved with the flight program
was Minnie Cole Savage (now Mrs. Duncan Cocke), a long
time resident of Williamsburg who was the only woman on
campus to solo. She gave up her flying career after
graduation in 1933.

The City of Williamsburg was quick to observe the
aviation activity at the college and bought a tract of
land west of town for an airport. It was leased to
William and Mary and a hanger was built. It was called
Scott Field. The college later bought its own tract a
few miles further west at Ewell which was called College
Field. However, with the death of President Chandler in
1934 interest in aviation began to decline and it is
believed that the high cost finally killed the program.

This chapter will close with some account of the well-known Dean, J. Wilfred Lambert. He came to William and Mary as a student in 1924 with a special introduction to President Chandler from ex-Governor Westmoreland Davis. Chandler got Lambert a job in the college dining hall waiting on tables. He also was responsible for another job with L. B. Ferguson in his Print Shop. After graduation he taught at Johns Hopkins but at Chandler's invitation returned to William and Mary to teach psychology. He continued to teach long after he became Dean of Men.

Dean Lambert has a phenomenal memory and can remember the details of his college days as well as the way Williamsburg was when he arrived. He remembers most of the businesses and buildings along Main Street as well as the old timers who ran them such as Bob Wallace, Billy Person, Archie Brooks, and Polly Stryker.

Because Lambert was a dean so long he was in the thick of projects and problems and can tell many tales about the people and events thereof.

Some of his earliest tales go back to President Lyon Tyler and Dr. Lesslie Hall. The latter, grandfather of our present Channing Hall, Jr., taught English and history, was dean of the faculty and assistant to President Tyler. Dr. Hall taught from 1888 to his death in 1928.

Some of Lambert's tales of these two include Henry Billups, long time Negro employee of the college. Since Henry drank, Dr Hall once said he was professor of "boozology." President Tyler fired Henry several times but always took him back since he performed his duties so well. Once Tyler fired him and then after trying to get into the Wren Building and finding it locked, rehired Billups to get the building open.

Another time Tyler asked Henry to find out the time from the college sundial. "But its night time," said Henry. "Then take a lantern," replied Tyler. Tyler, who was quite absent-minded, once went to Richmond, taking two of his children along. He returned without them and when his wife asked where they were he replied, "I left them standing on the corner of Seventh and Main in Richmond."

In 1938 Henry Billup's fiftieth anniversary was observed by a presentation of a watch to him with a chain, holding a small bell on one end. This was to recognize Henry's ringing the college bell in the Wren Building for so many years. After the presentation, Henry came to the lectern to make an acceptance speech. He thanked everyone present and started to leave the stage amid much applause, but he thought of something else to say and came back to the lectern to tell how nice everyone was to him, etc. Again he left amid applause and again returned. This was repeated several times and the applause was less each time. It seems that Henry had fortified himself with strong drink against the rigors of acceptance and had slightly overdone it.

John D. Rockefeller gave him an exceptionally good price for a house he owned on Henry Street, since Dr. Goodwin told Rockefeller he was such a fine citizen. Henry then built a house on Armistead Avenue to rent to a faculty member but he liked it so well that he decided to live in it himself.

In spite of stepping over the boundaries of propriety a few times, Henry Billups rendered unusually long and faithful service to William and Mary. He was first hired in 1888 by Tyler and retired in 1951 after 63 years on the job. However, the Governor of Virginia wrote a letter saying that because of Henry's long service he was to be retained. So he never actually retired but received full pay until he died in 1955.

Wren Building — 1931                    "Barrett Beach"

Chapter 10

EASTERN STATE HOSPITAL

Previous mention has been made of my home's nearness to the hospital and I was well aware of its impact on the community. Most Williamsburgers were aware of the hospital's effect on the town since it covered so much of our real estate and afforded employment to a good number of our citizens.

I became somewhat familiar with the hospital at an early age and sometimes strolled through the grounds with my brothers or sister. We talked to the patients and sometimes ran errands for them, usually to the stores uptown for gum or candy. Occasionally we watched their dances through the windows of Cameron Hall and later we watched movies from the doors which were left open in warm weather. From Cameron Hall westward to Henry Street there was an iron fence. From this fence eastward was a high board fence which enclosed the exercise yard for the women patients. It was through the boards in this fence that we got to know some of the female patients and passed the things we bought for them. Two of them I remember in particular were Mrs. Upton who was very ladylike and one we called "Chew Tabicca." She sometimes talked to trees on the grounds and this was the only thing she said that we could understand from her muttering. She would repeat "Chew Tabicca" over and over.

This is not to say that we made the hospital grounds our playground. We had been made well aware of the nature of the hospital through parental warnings, an occasional word from a nurse or attendant and especially from the shouts and moans of the more disturbed patients, more often at night. This combined with the somber atmosphere pervading the hospital and kept us

Eastern State Entrance on Francis Street

from becoming overly familiar with the place.

The parents of some of my schoolmates worked at Eastern State Hospital and through them I felt some of the stigma attached to the hospital. It was more felt than expressed and not everyone felt or recognized it. However, there were those who felt it to such a degree that they were reluctant to admit having worked there in their youth, especially if they attained some degree of success in business in later years.

Eastern State, as long-time residents of Williamsburg call the hospital, is the oldest institution in the United States dealing solely with mental illness. Its history has been written repeatedly. A brief outline of it here will be given for the benefit of those who may not have encountered it heretofore.

Establishment of the hospital was at the instigation of Governor Francis Fauquier who urged the creation of "a hospital---for the reception of those

who are so unhappy as to be deprived of their reason."
He first brought up the subject in the House of
Burgesses in 1766 and in 1770 they passed an act estab-
lishing a "Public Hospital for Persons of Insane and
Disordered Minds." The institution opened in 1773.

Fauquier was one of Virginia's better governors,
whose career was marked by his struggle to provide com-
passion to his people through their government.

James Galt was offered the position of keeper.
He was the first of the remarkable Galt family who held
positions of leadership at the hospital for 89 consecutive
years. He called upon Dr. John de Sequeyra (pronounced
Se-quar-ya) to see each patient upon admission and thus
he became the first visiting physician.

James Galt's brother, Dr. John M. Galt was
appointed visiting physician in 1795 and upon James
death in 1800 his son William T. Galt became keeper.
Dr. John M. Galt was succeeded by his son, Alexander D.
Galt. Alexander's son John M. Galt II became the first
superintendent in 1841. This position combined the
duties of keeper and visiting physician. His service
ended in 1862 when union forces invaded Williamsburg
under General George McClellan. Galt died of a heart
attack a few days later. He had been totally dedicated
to the care of the mental patients and was one of the
first to recognize the value of occupational therapy
and recreation in their treatment.

First called the Hospital for Idiots and Lunatics,
the name was changed in 1841 to Eastern Lunatic Asylum
and in 1894 it received its present name.

Eastern State Hospital was planned by Peyton
and John Randolph, John Blair Jr., Thomas Everard and
other distinguished colonial citizens and this is the
type of men who were on the board of directors through
the years. Some of them were: Dr. T. G. Peachy (1817-
1841), Dr. Jessie Cole (1826), Robert Saunders Jr.
(1831-1851). Robert H. Armistead (1851-1855), Richard
Bucktrout (1892-1898), Dr. Littleberry Foster (1892-
1898). Dr. Jessie Cole and Dr. Littleberry Foster were
keeper and superintendent respectively and were ancestors of H. D. Cole and Merritt Foster, our long-time
postmaster. Dr. Foster was superintendent from 1899 to
1907.

The first superintendent I remember was Dr. George W. Brown who held the position from 1911 to 1943. As children we first thought of him as the chief jailor but as we grew older and learned that the patients were treated kindly, we realized that Dr. Brown and his staff were dedicated to helping the patients to recover.

Treatment of the mentally ill made steady advancement under the administration of Dr. Brown which lasted longer than any other superintendent. He made improvement in the treatment and facilities. He stopped the use of hypnotics and alcoholic beverages. He was the first to impose strict sanitary regulations and he segregated patients suffering infectious diseases. In 1921 the lab equipment was improved and in 1923 the department of occupational therapy was added. In 1930 the patients numbered 1773, up from 600 in 1898.

When Dr. Brown became superintendent in 1911 the Steward was Archer Brooks who founded the Brooks Insurance Agency in 1890. The Clerk was John L. Mercer who had been Mayor from 1896 to 1904. The Engineer was R. B. Watts who founded Watts Motor Company in the early '30s. The hospital bought as many supplies from local merchants as possible. Some of them listed in annual reports of the period were: R. T. Casey & Sons, clothing, groceries and tobacco; Bozarth Brothers, railway rails and lumber; Galba Vaiden, ice; Mrs. W. H. Braithwaite, eggs, knives and forks. John H. Clowes was paid for returning an escaped patient and Thomas G. Peachy, postmaster, was paid rent for a Post Office box. Williamsburg's merchants could not supply all of the hospital's needs. One of the out-of-town merchants listed was Angelo Meyers who was paid $90.31 for whiskey. This was no doubt used in the treatment of some patients, a common practice until Dr. Brown put a stop to it sometime during his long administration.

Eastern State Hospital attracted doctors from far and wide and it is more than likely that Williamsburgers enjoyed better medical attention than they would have without the hospital. An example of the city's good fortune can be seen with the arrival of Dr. Baxter Bell Sr. whose dedication has already been described. He came to Eastern State in 1917 as assistant physician and was one of two physicians on the staff during the influenza epidemic of 1918. He remained until 1925 when he opened his practice in town at his home in the Carter-Saunders House on Palace Green. A year later he moved his home and practice to the former Williamsburg Hotel on Main Street near the Powder Horn, where he remained until 1930 when he built his own small general hospital on Cary Street.

Dr. John M. Henderson was another physician who was on the staff of Eastern State. He was mayor of Williamsburg from 1916 to 1928.

One of Eastern State's employees who worked there an uncommonly great number of years was Lawrence Caldwell. He came to work in 1928 and attended William and Mary while working. He started as a clerk and was promoted to steward which is equivalent to business manager. Before he retired in 1975 he was assistant director. The Administration Building is named in his honor.

The annual report of 1911 listed the occupations of the patients. Among the most numerous were laborers, clerks, carpenters, etc. Included on the list were one actress, five engineers, one cigarmaker, two harnessmakers, one horse trader, one lawyer, one stonecutter, one trunkmaker and one prostitute.

The nativity of the patients was also listed. Of course most of them were Virginians, with nearby states furnishing a good number each. Included on the list were five from Germany, three from Russia and one each from India and China.

The reports tell of the causes of hospitalization of the patients. Under the heading "Alleged Causes of Psychosis" were listed: Business worry-5, alcohol-33, family trouble-8, financial loss-2, masturbation-5, morphine-7, religion-2. Another list headed "Psychosis" included imbecility-17, idiots-4, paranoia-13, dementia praecox-17 and pallagrous insanity-6.

Some of the medical treatment listed in the early reports at the hospital were amputations, tonsilectomies, hemorrhoidectomies, deliveries and sterilization. In

1934 the latter was listed for 24 females and 14 males.
When I grew old enough to learn the facts of life, I
heard about sterilization and it seems that hospital
personnel and the average Williamsburger agreed that this
was the best thing to do to prevent the birth of mentally defective children to mental patients.

Dr. Brown was well known around town. I knew him
only slightly but I heard things about him. He apparently had a sense of humor. One time in the late '30s
when Fannie Nightengale was working at the Peninsula Bank
and Trust Co. on Main Street Dr. Brown told her that she
had developed quite a "Yankee accent." He prescribed
gargling to get rid of it.

In 1926 a new medical building was built on South
Henry Street and named "The Brown Building," to honor Dr.
Brown. I thought it was the best looking building of
them all and was sorry to see it demolished in the early
'70s. However, the new medical building at Dunbar was
also named for Dr. Brown so his memory is still perpet-
uated at Eastern State.

Dr. Brown taught clinical psychology at William
and Mary during the '20s. His daughter, Thelma, was also
on the faculty at that time, teaching Physical Education.
She later served as J.A.C. Chandler's secretary.

As mentioned previously, Dr. Brown was responsible for many of the improvements in treatment and facilities at the hospital but his administration was not
unmarred by problems. In September of 1930 a patient,
Percy Wilcox was forced into the "hot pack" bath by an
attendant. He was kept there for 30 minutes and when
taken out he collapsed into unconciousness. He died
that night. His father charged the hospital with
incompetency. The State Commissioner of Welfare ordered
an investigation. The conclusion was that Dr. Brown
and his staff had done the best that they could under
the circumstances. Both he and the Commissioner had
fought for additional funds to upgrade facilities and
personnel. Wages were always low at the hospital and
attendants of high quality could not be retained. Dr.
Brown stated in one of the annual reports of the '30s
that it was difficult to keep good attendants, even
during The Depression. The best were the first to
leave for better jobs.

The hospital maintained a farm from 1870 until recent years. It was located just south of the hospital grounds between Henry and South England Streets. It contained 170 acres. A large variety of produce was raised there as well as chickens and cattle for eggs, beef and milk. Dr. Brown wrote in the annual report of 1911, "The farm is in first class condition but is inadequate for our needs, still, it supplies us with vegetables." He recommended that $5,000. be spent on an addition to the farm. In 1919 he was responsible for the hospital buying the old Dunbar plantation for an extension of the farm; 486 acres were first purchased and the acreage was increased to 1300 later.

There was no further room for expansion of the hospital at the site on Francis Street and it was realized that further expansion would have to be at the Dunbar site. John D. Rockefeller could hear the crys of the more disturbed patients and suggested that they be moved to Dunbar to improve conditions for the tourists.

He speeded up the adoption of his suggestion by offering to help finance the move. In 1936 the first four buildings were constructed there. It was decided to move the entire hospital there eventually. The move was completed in 1970, when the last building on Francis Street was vacated.

The Rockefeller interests donated $25,000.00 towards accomplishing the move to Dunbar with the first four buildings being built between 1936 and 1938. The federal government appropriated $290,000.00 to help through the WPA.

When Dr. Brown retired in 1943 Dr. Joseph Barrett replaced him as superintendent. He had three sons who attended school with my brothers. One of them would visit Billy after school so I became acquainted with the family through him.

Dr. Barrett segregated patients into groups according to their condition. Some of these were listed as Bed-infirm, Ambulatory-old age, Continuous treatment-quiet, Deteriorated, Chronic disturbed and Convalescent.

He presented statistics about the hospital in his reports, giving a possible explanation for there being more female patients than male. He believed that men were a better economic asset to the family than women and were therefore kept at home longer. In 1945 he wrote that the furlough rate of men and women was about equal.

Through the years as the hospital was slowly moved to Dunbar it was understood that William and Mary would get most of the land for its future expansion. Colonial Williamsburg wanted some of the area for possible reconstruction of colonial buildings. By 1953 a great controversy had developed between C.W. and the college. However, by 1960 it became quite clear that William and Mary would expand to the west and would not need any more of the Eastern State land. (The college uses a former dairy barn for its endocrinology lab.)

C.W. then was able to buy the two parcels of land it wanted. One was the Travis Tract on the northeast corner of Francis and Henry Streets, now containing the Travis House, the former superintendent's house and the former site of the Executive Building. For this they paid $116,400.00. The other parcel called the Custis Tract on the south side of Francis Street, goes from the Custis Kitchen to the corner of Francis and Henry Streets. For this the college received $605,000.00. Both sums were to be used for the construction of the new Swem Library. The three powers are said to have negotiated in a most cooperative fashion and the results were deemed highly beneficial to all. Colonial Williamsburg decided to reconstruct the original hospital building and at this writing archeological excavation and study is still being done.

Courtesy of Mr. Martin Kline

Eastern State aerial view — about 1935

Chapter 11

ODDS AND ENDS

This chapter is called "Odds and Ends" because I think it sounds better than "miscellaneous." Such a chapter is needed to discuss aspects of the Williamsburg scene not covered in the foregoing pages. It covers briefly such topics as clubs, churches and Black people. Unfortunately, I haven't collected enough information on any one of these to write a separate chapter. It seemed advantageous to collect this information in a catch-all chapter with which to end this book. One of its advantages is that information could be added at the last minute without disrupting any of the preceeding pages.

## WILLIAMSBURG BAPTIST CHURCH

Williamsburg Baptist, the church in which I was baptized as a teenager, was formed in 1829 but the ground work was laid much earlier. A Baptist church had been in James City County since 1773. First called "Zion Baptist Church," the name was changed to Williamsburg Baptist Church in 1856.

The first pastor was Reverend Scervant Jones who is buried beside his wife, Ann Timson Jones, in Bruton churchyard. His tombstone extols his kindness and zeal for the Baptist cause. His wife preceeded him in death and is described by the Rev. Jones as having adored her husband and having all the graces. Reverend Jones was educated as a lawyer but gave up his practice to enter the ministry. The "Old Powder Horn" was used as his church. It had a gallery which was used by the colored members, as was the case at Bruton. Reverend Jones died in 1854 but he saw the cornerstone of a new church laid facing Main St. near the Powder Horn. The wall around the latter was torn down to be used in the foundation of the new church.

The pastor of Williamsburg Baptist Church when I first attended in the early '30s was Reverend W.C James who remained through the move to Richmond Road in 1934. In 1937 he was succeeded by Dr. Carter Helm Jones. In 1942 Reverend Archie F. Ward Jr. was called and remained until 1952 when he resigned to become the chaplain of Eastern State Hospital. The Reverend Thomas E. Pugh assumed the leadership of the church after Rev. Ward and retired in January 1981.

Some of the members of the 1934 building committee were: Mrs. F. R. Ayers, Dr. D. J. Blocker, Mr. and Mrs. J. A. Bozarth, Dr. George Brown, Mr. C. T. Casey, Dr. J. A. C. Chandler, Mrs. M. W. Foster, Dr. J. R. Geiger, Miss Helen Graham, Dr. J. R. L. Johnson, Mr. J. F. Lanford, Gov. John G. Pollard, Mrs. H. M. Stryker, Mrs. John Taylor and Mr. J. S. Timberlake.

## FIRST BAPTIST CHURCH

In the same year in which Williamsburg Baptist Church was completed, 1855, a new church for Negro Baptists was built on Nassau Street as has been previously mentioned. The first colored worshipers attended services in Bruton Parish but were allowed only to sit in the north gallery. As Baptists gained strength and numbers after the Revolution, colored worshipers met at Green Spring Plantation in James City County and with the permission of their masters they built a temporary shelter or "brush arbor" at Green Spring. Later one was built at Raccoon Chase between Williamsburg and Jamestown. Around 1776 they moved to Williamsburg and in 1791 became the First Baptist Church. They were first led by a man called Moses and then by Gowan Pamphlet.

This church has been called the first Negro church in the country but like so much early history is difficult to document. The few available records are not complete and are mixed with legend. After Gowan Pamphlet died the congregation disintegrated for a few years and mixed with white congregations. As mentioned, Scervant Jones preached

Courtesy of Daily Press

First Baptist Church — Nassau Street

to a mixed congregation. The church was revived as First
Baptist Church and later Robert P. Cole allowed them to
use his carriage house on Nassau Street where the first
permanent church was built.

In 1956, the church moved into a new building on
Scotland Street. Colonial Williamsburg bought the old one.

## MT. ARARAT BAPTIST CHURCH

Another colored Baptist church of which I was at
least somewhat aware for many years was Mt. Ararat. When
I worked in the A & P store before World War II I met its
pastor, the Reverend Lewis Wales, Jr. He was a stout
man and walked with a limp. I don't ever remember seeing
him smile so I concluded that he was a very serious man.

Mt. Ararat Baptist Church was established in 1882
and built on Francis Street. The first pastor was C. H.
Garlick. He resigned after two years and in 1885 Lewis
W. Wales was called a few months before his graduation

from Richmond Institute, later called Virginia Union
University. He remained pastor of Mt. Ararat and several
other small Negro churches in the area until he died in
1927. His son, Lewis W. Wales, Jr., was then called to
be the pastor of Mt. Ararat.

Lewis Wales, Sr. acquired extensive real estate
in and around Williamsburg and the family home was on
Francis Street near the present site of Williamsburg Inn.
In 1933, the wooden church on Francis Street was replaced
by the present brick structure on the corner of Franklin
and Botetourt Streets. Since the death of Lewis Wales,
Jr., in 1966 the pastor has been Reverend James B. Tabb.

## ELDER MICHAUX

Sometime in my youth I became aware of Elder
Michaux and his Church of God. It was not until the
completion of the Colonial Parkway to Jamestown in 1957
that I saw his Gospel Spreading Farm on the north side of
the parkway and the amusement park across the road. It
was then that I began to understand somewhat the proportions
of his enterprises.

Elder Lightfoot Solomon Michaux (pronounced Mee-Shaw)
was a colored native of Buckroe in the present city of
Hampton. He spent his youth on the Peninsula and established his first mission in Newport News before World War
I. He established churches in several states and made his
headquarters in Washington D.C. It was from here that he
directed his Gospel Spreading Association through which
he became involved in several large real estate projects.

He began to broadcast the gospel early in Newport
News and continued this practice in Washington in later
years. He became acquainted with important people in such
varied fields as government and entertainment.

In 1936, he bought over 1,000 acres fronting on the
James River close to Jamestown. This land was purchased
from Thomas S. Brabrand under the name of "The National
Memorial to the Progress of the Colored Race in America,
Inc." The acreage was formerly known as "Spratley's."
On this land he established the James City County Bible
and Agriculture Training School which became the Gospel
Spreading Farm as it is today.

The National Park Service tried unsuccessfully to condemn part of Michaux's land along the river in 1941 in order to continue the parkway to Jamestown. However, he later sold the Park Service enough land for the road for $10,000.00.

Michaux had great plans for this land on the James River but they were never completed. His efforts in Washington and elsewhere were more fruitful, leading to the building of several large housing developments. He died in 1968.

## SAM HARRIS

I can remember only one blacksmith during my growing years in Williamsburg. He was a colored man named Sam Harris. He first kept a shop to the rear of the Methodist Church and later moved to "The Triangle." This is an area of shops bounded by Armistead Avenue, Prince George and Scotland Streets. It was a Negro area during the '30s and '40s.

Sam was known as a good person and was good at his trade, but he was easily persuaded and therefore was not a good businessman. He made "good" money but lost most of it. Jeff Carter, one of my

Courtesy of Daily Press

Sam Harris — Blacksmith

schoolmates, remembers that Sam made tools for his
father, who was a brickmason.

There was another colored Sam Harris who
lived in Williamsburg, but it was in the last century. He died in 1904. He operated a general store
on the corner of Main and Botetourt Streets. He was
better known than the blacksmith. He apparently
was a good businessman since he owned a great deal of
property in and out of Williamsburg.

## STREET NAMES

A few words must be written about the street
names in Williamsburg. Before the town was restored,
most of the streets were sparsely marked, if at all,
and they were sometimes called by other than their
duly-registered names.

As stated throughout this narrative, Duke of
Gloucester was called "Main Street" by most of the
residents. In recent years, some college students
have called it "DOG Street" from its initials, but
this has never been widespread. Older residents
remember when Francis and Nicholson Streets were
referred to as "Back Streets" in the '20s. In 1932,
when Williamsburg Steam Laundry was moved from the
future Palace grounds to Boundary Street, the short
intersecting street with Boundary Street was called
Northington Street. Today, the C&P Telephone Company
building sits on this corner and Northington is part
of Lafayette Street. Palace Street was sometimes
known as Tyler Street and Dunmore was called
Spottswood before its original name was restored.
York Street was called Woodpecker Street.

Before the Capitol was restored in the early
'30s, that end of Main Street forked into two streets.
Blair to the right or south was at about a 100-degree
angle, not 90 degrees as today. The other fork to the
left or north was called Capitol Street and departed
from Main at about a 120-degree angle.

Soon after coming to Williamsburg, Professor
Woodbridge moved to Texas Avenue. A short while
later, the name of the street was changed to Griffin
Avenue. Cary Street was Oklahoma Avenue.

Ireland Street, for those unfamiliar with the town, is one block long running from Boundary to Henry Street, south of Francis Street. Apparently, this street once continued through Eastern State property and crossed England Street. "Professor" Charles inferred as much in his writings, and a 1930s map shows a short street going east from England Street in the area of the present day Craft House parking lot.

Mr. Charles wrote about Richmond and Jamestown Roads in Civil War times. In those days, Richmond Road was called "Stage Road" and Jamestown Road was known as the "Mill Road."

Ewell Street was a short street between Scotland and Railroad Street with Dunmore to the west and England Street on the east. King Street was between Nassau and England going from Main to Francis Street (see map).

## THE PULASKI CLUB

Williamsburg has a unique club which has had no indoor quarters since 1939. It is one of the oldest social clubs in the nation. Only the Old Colony Club in Boston claims to be older, having been founded in 1769. The Pulaski Club dates back to 1777 according to its members but it was called "The Pulaski Club" in 1779 to honor Count Casimir Pulaski who died in that year. He fought for this country in the Revolutionary War under George Washington who expressed a desire for such a club and mentioned "The Club" in his writings. The club was organized at the Raleigh Tavern and met there during its early days.

The membership was once held to 20 but now allows 29 which is the age of Pulaski when he died. New members are accepted to replace older ones only when death creates a vacancy.

I became aware of this club sometime in my youth when I developed curiosity about the benches in front of the old Cole Shop. I was told it was the meeting place of a club where a bunch of old fogeys loafed. The benches have always been the outdoor meeting place of the club.

I remember Mr. Henry Dennison Cole and his shop

where books, newspapers and post cards were sold.  It was
around the block from where I lived on Francis Street.
I remember a bulletin board nailed to a tree in the vicinity
of the benches.  News of the town and the college was
dutifully posted by Mr. Cole.  The club met in the back of
his shop in cold weather until 1939 when the Restoration
bought the building.  The back room where meetings were
held was removed since it was not part of the original
building.

The club almost faded out of existence during the
Civil War but was revived in the 1870s.  Den Cole, as he
was called, was a guiding light of the old club.  There
is evidence from his writings that he is responsible for
reviving the club, probably while attending the college
from 1870 to 1875.  It seems that the club moved with him
to his shop and has been in it and in front of it since
that time.  Of course it no longer consists of college
boys but older gentlemen, most of whom are retired.  One
of the requirements of membership is to be a good loafer.
Another requirement is to be a good story teller.  Members

Courtesy of Dr. Carlton Casey

Pulaski Club — early 30s — "Den Cole" holding great-nephew Vernon Geddy, Jr.

are selected from "interlopers," those who join members
on the benches for indeterminate periods. If accepted, one
is asked to join, but the club seldom does anything in a
hurry. Some interlopers have waited for as long as 15
years before being asked to join. The initiation fee is a
quart of Virginia Gentleman and the certificate of membership is an Octagon Soap wrapper with the member's name and
date of admission on the back. The only dues are paid
when a member dies-for a memorial. Any left over money is
put in a fund to be used for an occasional banquet.

Members have included some of the town's most
distinguished citizens. In Den Cole's latter days, he
was Secretary-Treasurer. The President was John S.
Charles; Vice-President, Spencer Lane. The Sergeant-
at-Arms was "Red-Headed" Jim Bowry and the Chaplain
was the Reverend E. Ruffin Jones. Some of the other
members were J. Spafford Timberlake, R. W. Kyger,
L. B. Ferguson, J. T. Blacknall, Archie Brooks, Marston
Christian, Boyd Creasy, Professor T. J. Stubbs and
Judge Frank Armistead. Most of them served in the above-
mentioned positions of leadership at one time or another.

John D. Rockefeller, Jr. was accepted as a member
and he cherished his certificate of membership enough to
place it with his art treasures. In 1935 he donated
new benches to the club since the old ones were falling
apart. The club wrote one of their rare letters to thank
him for his kindness. In 1952 Rockefeller sent a letter
expressing regret at not being able to attend a supper
honoring the late Judge Frank Armistead. It was sent to
Bob Kyger on Duke of Gloucester Street.

Among the more recent members were Dr. Henry Davis,
Ellsworth Ayers, Drewry Jones, Edgar Wells, George
Williams, Lloyd Williams and Herbert Ganter.

Among the few honorary members have been Robert S.
Bright , Bela Norton and the Honorable A. J. Montague,
former Governor of Virginia and member of Congress. The
only female to be an honorary member is Caroline Geddy
Frechette, sister of our recent mayor, Vernon Geddy.
She was accorded the honor in 1936 because she was the
great niece of Den Cole.

As in most organizations, only the "faithful few"
are active, but today the club is still strong and interest
remains high.

## KING'S DAUGHTERS

The oldest organization in Williamsburg for women is the Kate Custis Circle of the King's Daughters. It was formed in 1888 by Miss Catherine Wharton Custis, who was called Kate. She was asked to form the circle by Mrs. Isabella Davis, one of the charter members of The International Order of King's Daughters and Sons. Mrs. Davis met Kate Custis in 1887 when she visited Williamsburg. The circle was later named after Kate, who was the first president. The earliest records have been lost. The existing ones date back to 1913 and they show that there were 33 members. In 1947, there were 60 members.

The Kate Custis Circle of the King's Daughters is a charitable organization and has quite a record of public service. Their contributions have included donations to crippled children, a boys' home, and Christmas boxes to the sick and poor.

When Kenneth Chorley was asked for a donation to the King's Daughters in 1933, he inquired about the organization and he said he was told that the circle was the only charitable organization in Williamsburg. They can stretch a dollar farther than anyone. They cooperate with the State Health Department, the Juvenile and Domestic Relations Court, the American Red Cross, the Virginia Tuberculosis Association, and the James City Welfare Board. They procure rooms and buy groceries for the needy and furnish lunches and glasses for needy children. Everyone in Williamsburg supports the King's Daughters.

Parkway Tunnel
Under Construction — 1940

Audrey House (Brush-Everard)
before Restoration

Knitting Mill on
Railroad Avenue — 1890s

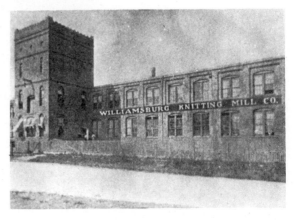

## Some Williamsburg Landmarks

# Index